Freight Weather
The Art of Stalking Trains

Photography and text by

D. C. JESSE BURKHARDT

Copyright © 2001

"SCENIC STOP"
Union Pacific Railroad
Modoc Line
Ambrose, California
June 1998

*Crossbucks and a stop sign mark an obscure crossing
on the former SP Modoc Line.*

For Leslie and Clare

"SLOW BRANCH"
Southern Pacific Railroad
Bailey Branch
Alpine Junction, Oregon
February 18, 1988

SD9 #4431 swings past the decrepit 10 mph speed board that marks the junction of the Bailey Branch and the West Side Branch. The crew of the Dawson Local is headed north to Corvallis with six loads of lumber -- two woodchip cars and four flats -- retrieved from the Hull-Oakes Lumber Company sawmill a few miles away at Dawson. Soon the hogger will notch up #4431 to 25 mph as it regains the West Side Branch, just a few yards ahead.

Train Stalking

" *Stalking trains is a form of emotional healing as well as a spiritual practice. Because of the aloneness, the self-honoring, and there is something timeless about it. It's a fabulous metaphor for the difficult art of staying in the present. The present is what you find when the train finally shows up, and its thunder stops your world. And the weedy trackside spots where you walk or wait represent the beauty and the potential that is always around us, but unseen by the daily mind.* "

— Paulette K. Pollard, Seattle, Washington, March 1998

"BACKING HOME"
Mount Hood Railroad
Hood River, Oregon
May 27, 1998

An excursion train on the Mount Hood Railroad's Hood River-Parkdale line backs around a curve into the shortline's three-track switching yard.

Table of Contents

Preface ——————————————————————————— 13

I: COLUMBIA RIVER GORGE: WATER COLORS ————— 21
The Celilo Wind ————————————————— 23
Heartbeat of the Gorge ——————————————— 24

II: HEARTLAND: DREAMS OF THE UPPER MIDWEST ——— 49
In Hemingway Country ——————————————— 51
Free River ————————————————————— 53
'61 Valiant ———————————————————————— 57

III: THE WEST COAST: ROLLING IMAGES ——————— 65
Shelter —————————————————————————— 66
Visions Of Responsibility ——————————————— 68

IV: POSTCARDS FROM CANADA ——————————— 103
Blood Hunger ——————————————————— 105

Epilogue ——————————————————————— 117
On the Bridge, Gone ——————————————— 119

"OKLAHOMA STEAM"
Union Pacific Railroad #8444
Peckham, Oklahoma
February 1968

Collection of Gaylord Aylesworth

Never has man

"Never has man produced a more

lonely sound than the whistle of

a steam locomotive. It was a sad

sound that seemed to say to each

of us who heard it: Come with me

and I'll show you America. Follow

me all the days of your life, and

as you lie down to die, you'll

pray with your last breath

to follow me once again. "

— Ralph Goodings, *"A Book of Traveler's Tales"*

"HEADLAMP RISING"
Willamette & Pacific Railroad
Newberg District
Sherwood, Oregon
July 3, 1994

West of Sherwood, Oregon, a southbound Willamette & Pacific Railroad freight rises up from between the trees in the distance. The train is moving scrap steel to the Cascade Steel Rolling Mills plant in McMinnville, along a shaky roadbed that is obviously in need of a section gang. The trackage is known as the Newberg Branch, which begins at Cook and terminates in St. Joseph, a few miles south of Newberg. The W&P took over operations along the former Southern Pacific route in February 1993.

"NO LOITERING"
Willamina & Grand Ronde Railroad
Willamina, Oregon
May 1997

Preface

"Learn patience ... then haul."

— Somewhere along the Mississippi River, near Winona, Minnesota, May 1977

What intrigues me about railroads? The roots of the interest in "stalking trains" are difficult to explain, except by relating some personal history.

I grew up in Jackson, Michigan, and lived in a quiet suburban neighborhood less than a mile from a New York Central (later Penn Central) mainline. The tracks and the trains that hustled along that line were frequently in my consciousness. Especially at night, when there were few other distractions, I could clearly hear the air horn warnings as trains approached two distant road crossings. Some still evenings, I could even hear the delicate sound of the crossing bells ringing through the darkness as I rested by my open bedroom window.

It was the sound of the railroad night, and it conjured up mysteries that have never left my spirit: I wondered where the trains were going; I imagined their westward routes across the Midwestern plains and pictured far off railroad scenes.

Eventually I found out that the long westbounds were on their way to a modern classification yard in Elkhart, Indiana. The eastbounds stopped in Jackson's freight yard. There, cuts of cars would be set out for local switching operations, while through trains would be reconfigured before going on toward Detroit with a new crew.

Jackson was a major railroad hub when I was a kid. Take a look at a map from the early 1950s, and that tells the tale. There were no fewer than eight rail routes radiating out of Jackson. Seven of them were NYC lines, while Grand Trunk

Western owned the other.

The GTW line went northeast toward Pontiac and Port Huron, while the NYC lines went just about everywhere: to Ann Arbor and Detroit; to Manchester and Tecumseh and on to Toledo, Ohio; to Cement City and Hudson and later to a connection with the Wabash at Alvordton in northern Ohio; to Jonesville and Reading and on to Fort Wayne, Indiana; to Homer and Three Rivers and on to Elkhart; to Albion, Kalamazoo and Chicago; and to Rives Junction and, beyond there, to either Lansing or Grand Rapids. The possibilities appeared endless.

But of course it couldn't last. By the late 1980s, five of those eight lines were ancient history.

As in the rest of the country, rapid changes have swept over Michigan's rail network in the last few decades. In fact, if I were to put a personal timeline to what took place in my hometown, it would read like this: When I was born, the Jackson to Elkhart mainline near my home in Jackson was owned by New York Central. When I was 15 years old, Penn Central inherited the line. Conrail ran the trains when I was 23. By the time I turned 30, the line had been taken out of service. When I marked my 32nd birthday, the rails and ties were gone, and only a dirt trail remained to remind local residents of a once-busy freight corridor.

"Unnecessary mileage," a Conrail spokesman said at the end. Now, with its 1999 division between CSX and Norfolk Southern, apparently Conrail itself is considered "unnecessary."

The first time I saw an abandoned track was in the mid-1960s. It was just west of Jackson, and it was night; maybe that added an extra element of wonder. I was 10 or 12 years old, and a couple of neighborhood buddies and I were riding our bikes eastward on a dirt trail alongside the main NYC line out of town. In the moonlit darkness, we noticed a paralleling rail line coming in from the southwest. What a wonderful surprise! As we continued to follow the converging routes, however, I was shocked to see the rails of the paralleling track had been dismantled where they once had formed a connection with the NYC main. Later, I learned that it had been a secondary NYC route, which had branched off at that desolate point and cut straight to Fort Wayne.

I couldn't figure out why those tracks had been removed. I even wondered if they were being worked on, and the dismantling was a temporary situation. It was a mystery; it seemed totally illogical and bizarre -- and it does to this day, actually. There's something staggering about the finality of that type of change.

In fact, I believe that some of the most poignant scenes I've photographed feature abandoned tracks. It can be a haunting image. What a tale those lush weeds could tell ...

Looking back at those not-so-distant times when I lived in Michigan, imagine the unbelievable changes I could have captured with a good camera. But as a youth, photography was unimportant, and in any case, it seemed like freight trains would *always* be hauling goods back and forth on that main track between Jackson and Elkhart.

Although I lived for almost 20 years near an active mainline -- about five through freights ran daily on the Elkhart-Jackson route -- I hold more appreciation for backwater feeders and shortlines as opposed to heavy-duty mainlines. And I've always appreciated seeing a freight train infinitely more than a passenger train.

I can't rationalize that preference. It's just there.

During my years in Michigan, there was another line I developed an affection for: the Ann Arbor Railroad's route between Toledo, Ohio, and Elberta, Michigan. The 300-mile line cut northwest from Toledo and across Michigan, terminating at the railroad's carferry apron in Elberta, on the shore of Lake Michigan. As late as 1982, AARR ferries loaded with a couple dozen freight cars moved daily across the lake, westbound to Kewaunee (GB&W connection) and Manitowoc (Chessie System) in Wisconsin.

During the long summers, I often traveled to Lake Michigan, and in those years the red-orange locomotives of the Ann Arbor Railroad were a landmark of Michigan's north country. The tracks cut through some of the sweetest landscapes Michigan has to offer. Its rails wound through the sand dunes around Yuma and the forests around Mesick; crossed the Chesapeake & Ohio diamond at Thompsonville; rolled over the water of Betsie Bay on a low trestle just outside of Frankfort. Finally the rails butted up against the ferry docks at Elberta's Lake Michigan harbor, literally heading off over the water. The freight yard at Elberta was situated mere yards from the waves of the big lake.

A few miles out of Frankfort was the Betsie Bay campground. Now and then on summer nights I camped there in a sleeping bag, no tent even; I'd just throw my gear out under the endless stars and sleep in the short grass a few feet from the mainline of the AARR. Back in the early 1970s, one long train usually passed through in the middle of the night, heading into Elberta. Its baritone air horn in the distance would wake me, then soon the train would come hissing and clanking and squealing out of the darkness, and I'd watch until the faint lights of the caboose passed by, disappearing into the trees.

Like so many lines across North America, the Ann Arbor's route into Elberta has fallen silent. North of a sandpit at Yuma, 35 miles from Frankfort, the tracks have been out of service for several years. Another shortline, the Tuscola & Saginaw Bay Railroad, now carries traffic over the Ann Arbor-Yuma segment of the former Ann Arbor trunk line, approximately 220 miles. The Ann Arbor Railroad still exists, but only as a skeletal version of its former self: It survives today as a branch connecting Toledo and Ann Arbor, about 50 miles.

I left Michigan in the mid-1970s and headed west to live in Ashland, Oregon. At that time, Ashland offered a major presence by

Southern Pacific. It was just a small town near the lower portion of the Siskiyou Line, a secondary route that usually saw just one through train a day. But it compensated for its lack of activity by serving as a crew change point, and as a base for the helper units employed to push trains up and over the Siskiyou Mountain grades. Road locomotives assigned as helpers -- SD40s and SD45s, mostly -- idled in the Ashland yard at virtually all hours back then.

Nearly all of the railroad's presence in Ashland has since been eliminated. The crew sleeping quarters were torn down. The former depot was moved away from the tracks. The sanding towers and refueling bays were scrapped. The yard itself was reduced from multiple tracks to a single main and a couple of sidings. However, the Siskiyou Line itself -- now operated by the Central Oregon & Pacific Railroad -- still sees freight traffic on a daily basis. CO&P trains run over the Siskiyou Pass to and from a connection with UP's Shasta Line at Black Butte, California. The trains are not as long as in the SP years, but at least the sound of moving freight continues to reverberate through the mountains south of Ashland.

In 1977, after a few years in Ashland, I moved to Corvallis, in Oregon's Willamette Valley. It was another SP stronghold. Corvallis was a college town that happened to be situated at a crossing point of two vital SP branchlines: the north-south West Side Branch and the east-west Toledo Branch. Southern Pacific maintained a small freight yard in Corvallis, with a tiny yard office. A local crew operated north and south out of the yard five days a week. In addition to that traffic, through trains out of Eugene Yard rumbled through the quiet town seven days a week, on their way to and from a big Georgia-Pacific paper mill in Toledo, near the coast. And every evening, the *Philomath Local* out of nearby Albany would roll through on its way to serve area lumber mills and feed a steady supply of cars to the *Corvallis Local*.

At the time, the legions of SD9s pulling freights all around the Willamette Valley seemed almost boring. By the late 1990s, of course, spotting an SP SD9 at work would be only slightly less than a miracle. ("Barbasol green" Burlington Northern SD9s were only somewhat less rare, and a few, surprisingly, were even getting the new Burlington Northern Santa Fe paint, along with a rebuild.)

After a stay of a couple years in Corvallis, I moved to Salem, Oregon's state capital. There too, SP was the dominant railroad, with a significant presence by Burlington Northern as well. The SP line there was the heavy-duty main trunk known as the Valley Line, SP's primary north-south route from Portland to Los Angeles. Traffic was -- and remains -- very heavy, with many freight trains as well as the daily Amtrak *Coast Starlight* that links Seattle and Los Angeles. In addition, SP had an active freight yard in Salem that fed a handful of local fruit and vegetable packing plants and a few other shippers.

On BN's Oregon Electric Branch, meanwhile, a local worked north and south out of a small yard in Salem, and a daily hauler came through Salem each day, on its run between Albany and Vancouver, Washington.

Not too much has changed in the mainline schedule of trains in the Salem area as of the end of the 1990s, except, of course, it is now Union Pacific instead of Southern Pacific that operates the trains speeding along the Valley Line.

BNSF's branch, however, has undergone a weighty transformation. The former Oregon Electric interurban line is now segmented, and no longer do through trains with multiple locomotives pass through the Willamette Valley on their way north toward Vancouver. In 1995, BN finally negotiated trackage rights with SP and moved its through operations between Portland and Albany to the adjacent Valley Line. For a long time, BN had wanted to end through service on the northern reaches of the Oregon Electric route, due to the steep grades of Cornelius Pass southwest of Portland. Once BN gained access to the fast Valley Line, the Oregon Electric property was suddenly much less valuable to the carrier. It failed to make the cut as a feeder route, because there were few shippers along the northern portion of the line.

Enough freight traffic remained to attract a lean shortline, however: in the mid-1990s, a newly-formed company calling itself the Portland & Western Railroad (a sister of the Willamette & Pacific), began operating the former BN property north of Salem.

With Union Pacific's bigger capital budgets, there were supposed to be a number of capacity enhancements and line and yard upgrades in the West's rail network following its absorption of SP. To be sure, many major improvement projects were launched. For example, UP invested $38 million to rebuild SP's huge Roseville Yard in northern California, thereby increasing efficiencies and allowing "economically beneficial" consolidations -- including the substantial downgrading of Eugene Yard. Those enhancements are important to the efficient hauling of freight, perhaps, but nevertheless, a sense of history is being lost.

A night in early October 1996 was the first time I stood alongside Southern Pacific tracks following SP's September 12, 1996, absorption by Union Pacific. As I walked next to the rails at Oregon City, Oregon, on SP's sleek Valley Line, I noticed a light illuminating a string of boxcars next to the Smurfit paper mill there. In a moment, a fast, mixed freight came barreling around a corner, and as it swept up beside me, I was surprised to see a Union Pacific locomotive leading the way ... followed by two more UP units. It was sad to see SP's corporate image expunged so rapidly on what had been, for so many decades, SP's home turf.

Far worse, "rationalizations" spawned by the merger threatened to doom some lines.

In the West, one significant loss was expected to be SP's Modoc Line. The scenic route, which crosses the Warner Mountains in northern California, was scheduled to be severed between Wendel and Alturas, a distance of approximately 85 miles. UP's abandonment profile recommended that the line be removed from MP 445.6 to MP 360.1.

Although it now might be distant and forgotten, it wasn't all that long ago that the Denver & Rio Grande Western Railroad, following its purchase of SP in October 1988, reopened the Modoc Line, which had been temporarily closed to through traffic in a cost-cutting effort. Managers at D&RGW touted the rejuvenated Modoc Line as a great boon to shippers of lumber products, in Oregon in particular. Indeed, in 1988, Oregon's Public Utility Commission lauded the entry of D&RGW into Oregon as a "revitalizing" move for the state's shippers. In fact, the return of the Modoc Line, which would cut more than 250 miles off east/west routings, was spotlighted as one of the key benefits of the D&RGW/SP transaction.

SP's Modoc Line seemed to capture the essence of the carrier's long-haul freight activity. Crossing mountains and desert landscape on its run from Klamath Falls, Oregon, to Flanigan, Nevada, the rustic route symbolized Southern Pacific's rough-edged strategy. There wasn't much extra cash available for modernizing the line, but nevertheless, most of the time at least, trains continued to ply its sun-baked rails.

But everything has changed. Following UP's purchase of SP, there has been a fresh shift in thinking, and once again the Modoc Line is no longer regarded as necessary. Union Pacific shifted most of the traffic that traveled the route over to SP's Donner Pass line, or to the former Western Pacific route through Portola, California. UP has also considered moving Modoc Subdivision trains onto the Inside Gateway route between Klamath Falls, Oregon, and Keddie, California (via Bieber), using trackage rights over BNSF.

Even with the revitalization of certain Western rail routes and the increased frequency of freight traffic on many lines, there still exists a troubling trade off. For example, does additional freight traffic on the former SP line through Truckee, California, compensate for the loss of the magnificent Modoc Line, or the relative demise of Eugene Yard?

In August 1996, I was camping near the Modoc Line, somewhere north of Alturas, California. In the darkness, I heard the hiss and hum of SP helper units rolling light through the mountains. Hours earlier, in the middle of the hot day, those three locomotives had helped shove a long eastbound mixed freight over the Warner Mountain pass, near Likely, California. The crew must have stopped for a dinner break in Alturas, because it was well after dark when the trio of locomotives came through the night; running lights providing a slight illumination of their path as they cut around the winding, elevated grade through a pine forest on the other side of the valley.

It's probable that helpers will never be seen there again.

I landed in White Salmon, Washington, in late 1994, and that provided some visible relief from the UP/SP conundrum. BNSF's Fallbridge Subdivision mainline through the Columbia River Gorge features non-stop heavy activity, including everything from transcontinental trains to locals, from containers on flat cars to boxcars of lumber. Amtrak's *Empire Builder* is also a daily visitor. Compared to SP's Willamette Valley branchline traffic, it was akin to going from a rural, backwater railroad scene to a relative superhighway of freight trains.

Of course, right across the river, Union Pacific operates a parallel mainline that offers a virtual mirror image of BNSF activities. Locals, mixed merchandise trains, TOFC/COFC, and, until May 1997, Amtrak's *Pioneer* rode UP's Portland Subdivision rails through the Gorge.

But in my first visit to Lyle, Washington -- 10 miles east of White Salmon -- I was disheartened to see that BN's 42-mile Goldendale Branch had been removed. It represented the only pure freight branchline in the area, and the scenery of the canyon route the rails followed along the Klickitat River was awesome. I just missed it, too: the tracks had been pulled out in 1993-94.

Although the Mount Hood Railroad operates freight trains out of Hood River, Oregon, its operations are "diluted" by frequent excursion train service. Trains hauling exclusively freight are unusual, except in the dim light of the winter months.

Out of respect for all the varied and unpredictable rail exhibitions the North American continent has to offer, I've carried two Pentax K-1000s in my Ford truck almost constantly during the past few years. Usually, one camera has been loaded with Fuji Provia 100 or Kodachrome 64 slide film, with the other filled with black & white print film.

So here is "FREIGHT WEATHER," a chronicle of trains traveling through unconfined landscapes in diverse regions of the country. I have selected 120 images that, at least to my eyes, weave an elemental sense of the magic of the endless steel rails that link our communities and continue to touch our senses.

The brief anthology of essays and vignettes accompanying the photographs offer impressions of the power of love, travel, youth, freight trains, and the feeling of what it means to roll with unhindered passion through a world that demands compromise. The text is -- in the words of a close friend who shared many powerful railroad days -- "writing that celebrates the possibility and necessity of keeping faith with oneself."

Ultimately, the narrative is intended as a way to illustrate what it means to not only accept challenge, but to go looking for it -- even when the whole world wants to block your way.

— D. C. Jesse Burkhardt
White Salmon, Washington
October 21, 2000

"ABSOLUTE BLOCK"
Burlington Northern Santa Fe Railway
Oregon Trunk Subdivision
Terrebonne, Oregon
July 1997

"THE WARBONNET WAY"
Burlington Northern Santa Fe Railway
Fallbridge Subdivision
Home Valley, Washington
April 15, 1998

"PARTNERSHIP"
Union Pacific Railroad
Portland Subdivision
Rowena, Oregon
June 12, 1999

I Columbia River Gorge:
Water Colors

"
If you've ever heard the whistle of a fast freight train

Beating out a beautiful tune

If you've ever seen the cold blue railroad tracks

Shining by the light of the moon

If you've ever felt a locomotive shake the ground

I know you don't have to be told

Why I'm going down to the railroad tracks

And watch those lonesome boxcars roll.
"

— Butch Hancock, "Boxcars," Rainlight Music (ASCAP)

"INTO THE RIVER"
Burlington Northern Railroad
Fallbridge Subdivision
Bingen, Washington
March 21, 1991

Three miles east of Bingen, a derailment sent six grain cars into the Columbia River. The cost of cleanup and track repair hit $250,000, but there were no injuries. A broken rail was the apparent culprit.

The Celilo Wind

A primordial force carved this gorge
And washed unnamed mountains
To the ocean.

For generations and generations
The ancient ones made their longhouses
Near the edge and walked beside whitewater
When the river was free.

Wild salmon fairly boiled and churned
Where the roaring waters plunged: Wy-am!

Men walked their own planks
To dip the treasured fish out
With their big alder hoop-nets or, sometimes,
To lose their balance into Wyam's waters
To lose their roar into Wy-am's roar,
Their blood and bones erased in Her careless wash.

A weary old river, now in shackles, has been
Trained to do tricks with tamed lightning
For new tribes who are blind to magic,
For generators and generators.

Humiliated, only She knows this:
Her strength could rend the chains

But on lonely winter nights,
Out where the biggest dam shines
Like a mere birthday candle small and lost
In the vast frosty desert,
She weeps.

— Marc Baber, Eugene, Oregon, November 1997

HEARTBEAT *of* the Gorge

If you have a heart, how can you not like many things about the Columbia River Gorge? When the sky turns turquoise at night and the constellations begin to appear in the darkening sky with no big city glow to block out the endlessness of the universe, there is something you feel.

At dusk, you can see the snow and ice shining rosy on Oregon's Mount Hood, and then turn and look the other way and see Washington's Mount Adams in the dimming daylight.

There are so many obvious treasures: fascinating rivers, creeks, and waterfalls; hiking trails along moss-covered rocky cliffs; fresh snow in the hills; fog that clings wetly to the distant trees; coyotes yodeling wildly in the evening. And there is an ease of travel in much of the Gorge, as if it were a type of throwback zone, where traffic congestion is unusual, not an everyday expectation.

But there's something else unique to the region, and I think a lot of people miss it, or they fail to appreciate it: the remarkable heritage of the transportation network in the Columbia River Gorge. As it has for many decades, the area literally hums with the power of people and goods in transit. East and west, tugs and barges on the Columbia River constantly move woodchips and grain and a variety of container freight. East and west, trucks and autos ply the constantly active highways. East and west, two major railroads move a mix of merchandise -- everything from scrap steel to fresh fruit -- around the clock.

The railroads carry a sense of magic. The trains seem to connect in a spiritual way with the land, as if they belong there and have always been there: blasting out of raw, rock-faced tunnels, gliding under bridges, snaking along the edges of towns and along the river, always rolling somewhere distant; symbols of our national and international connectedness.

In Washington, trains operate along the Columbia River on a water-level route built in 1908. In its inception, the railroad doing the building was called the Spokane, Portland & Seattle Railway. The SP&S slogan was, "The Northwest's Own Railway."

Yes, the roots are deep, and they come with a subtle romance. The names on the multi-colored freight cars being steadily hauled through the Gorge carry poignant, mystical images of the wonders of North American geography. Take a look: *Pacific Fruit Express. Golden West Service. Montana Rail Link. Soo Line. Canadian Pacific. Cotton Belt. City of Prineville. Wisconsin Central. Cedar Rapids & Iowa City. Santa Fe. Denver & Rio Grande Western. Chicago & NorthWestern.*

And the rare, fading images of long-defunct carriers quietly reflect recent, dramatic changes in the West's transportation map: *Great Northern. Northern Pacific. Rock Island. Milwaukee Road. Seattle & North Coast.*

Seeing the names over distant years, I remember wanting to travel to those different places. Seeing the parade of trains now feeds a connection to the endless rails, rails that traverse the North American continent and could take a boxcar virtually anywhere. Steel links.

In the late 1990s and early 2000s -- as often as 30 times a day -- trains "race" other trains on opposite sides of the river: Union Pacific on the Oregon (south) shore; Burlington Northern Santa Fe on the Washington (north) shore. From Portland to Pasco, the rail lines run parallel, separated only by the wide river and the demands of competition. The result is an endless, fast flow of goods that offers a nice marketing edge to Northwest shippers ... and presents a paradise for photographers.

It's a bit rare nowadays when two major railroads exist basically side by side. Line abandonments and consolidations across the nation have reduced the once-common proliferation of parallel trackage. But that's definitely not the situation beside the waters of the Columbia River.

Burlington Northern Santa Fe and Union Pacific are the big players here, as they are throughout the West. Yet even the diminutive Mount Hood Railroad, based in Hood River, Oregon, is a key operator -- although sightseers have been the primary haulage in recent years. Trains on the Mount Hood line roll south from Hood River on a winding, switched-back route to Parkdale, passing all too many defunct fruit packing plants and lumber mills stilled by fires or economic troubles.

Even though Amtrak's *Pioneer* passenger train -- through Hood River and The Dalles, Oregon, on its way to and from Boise, Idaho, and Odgen, Utah -- passed from the landscape in 1997, passenger trains continue serving on the Washington side of the Columbia River Gorge. The *Empire Builder* follows a daily route from Vancouver to Spokane, then east through Idaho and Montana, cutting across the top of the nation through the grain belt Midwest, eventually going all the way to Chicago on a mainline that used to be owned by the appropriately-named Great Northern Railway.

In survivor's fashion, trains remain in the Columbia River Gorge. They endure. Their echoes still rumble in the hills; their distant horns call a signature "coming through" sound.

The rails run like bloodlines, tracing our heritage, creating the original foundation from where most of our cities would later develop: communities sprang up because the railroad went there.

The identification of the Gorge will forever interwine with the passage of colorful trains hauling a mixture of merchandise. There is a constant movement east and west, as if the whole nation was waiting on the goods blasting through: The heartbeat of the Gorge.

"PATIENCE"
Burlington Northern Santa Fe Railway
Wishram Subdivision
East Maryhill, Washington
October 19, 1996

On the siding at East Maryhill, Washington -- lost in the tremendous expanse of rocky bluffs along the Columbia River -- an eastbound Burlington Northern Santa Fe grain train headed by BN C30-7 #5081 waits, and waits, and waits still more. While this train idled on the side track, three westbound freights rolled past, and still the train sat, waiting for a green light.

"LANDFILL LOADS"
Burlington Northern Santa Fe Railway
Fallbridge Subdivision
Bingen, Washington
June 20, 1998

An eastbound trash train headed by BN GP50L #3131 moves through Bingen with loads bound for the regional landfill at Roosevelt, Washington.

"Z, CHRISTMAS EVE"
Burlington Northern Santa Fe Railway
Fallbridge Subdivision
Bingen, Washington
December 24, 1998

A hot BNSF "Z" intermodal train races west on a snowy Christmas Eve in the Columbia River Gorge.
The Z trains haul priority United Parcel Service trailers on an expedited schedule.

"SIDING TRIO"
Burlington Northern Santa Fe Railway
Fallbridge Subdivision
Cooks, Washington
March 10, 1999

Led by three locomotives nearly identical except for their paint schemes, a westbound BNSF freight blows past the siding at Cooks, Washington, behind freshly-painted SD40-2 #7001, SD40-2 #7040 in traditional BN colors, and Electro-Motive SD40-2 #6500.

"ROADWAY"
Union Pacific Railroad
Portland Subdivision
Rowena, Oregon
April 5, 1998

With the Columbia River on one side and the waters of Middleswart Lake on the other, a trainload of trailers heads eastbound near Oregon's Memaloose State Park. Pulling are UP C44-9W #9713, C&NW C44-9W #8636, and UP SD40-2 #3154.

"EASTWARD MIX"
Union Pacific Railroad
Portland Subdivision
Rowena, Oregon
April 5, 1998

Just minutes behind UP #9713 East, UP #6342 East follows with more trailers, powered by a sweet mixture of different locomotive types and road names. Behind UP SD60M #6342 are leased HLCX #6804 (in a shiny black paint that recalls the old New York Central), SP B39-8 #8000, and UP C41-8W #9406.

"LAST OF ITS KIND"
Union Pacific Railroad
DDA40X #6936
Portland Subdivision
Rowena, Oregon
October 25, 1997

Union Pacific's storied difficulties after absorbing Southern Pacific had at least one benefit: to help clean up a backlog of traffic, UP brought DDA40X #6936 out of mothballs. On October 25, 1997, #6936 heads a westbound stack train through the Columbia River Gorge near Rowena, Oregon, with an assist from UP SD40-2 #3766. UP's 6,600-horsepower #6936, built by EMD in 1971, is the last active one of its type on the UP system. A total of 47 of the huge locomotives were built.

"BACK IN TIME"
Mount Hood Railroad
Switchback, Oregon
February 4, 1999

It's 1999, but the carriers represented at the end of this short northbound freight on Oregon's Mount Hood Railroad -- a Western Pacific boxcar and a Great Northern caboose -- are throwbacks to the 1960s.

"BLOSSOM RUN"
Mount Hood Railroad
Pine Grove, Oregon
April 19, 1998

An excursion train on the Mount Hood Railroad comes through Pine Grove, Oregon, passing pear trees in bloom on one side and a siding for one of its vital freight customers on the other. The railroad carried approximately 40,000 passengers in 1997.

After Amtrak's eastbound Empire Builder has gone by, two "guest" Willamette & Pacific GP39-2s -- #2304 and #2307, both ex-Santa Fe -- come smoking out of the BNSF siding at Bingen, Washington, with a westbound rail train in August 1998. The W&P locomotives are named "Corvallis" and "Independence" in recognition of cities the W&P serves in Oregon's Willamette Valley.

"CORVALLIS AND INDEPENDENCE"
Willamette & Pacific Railroad
BNSF's Fallbridge Subdivision
Bingen, Washington
August 7, 1998

In an unusual sight, Canadian National #5621 is at the head of a "bare table" train rolling eastbound on BNSF rails in the summer of 1997.

"CANADIAN COLORS"
Burlington Northern Santa Fe Railway
Fallbridge Subdivision
North Dalles, Washington
August 1997

"TWIN SILVER"
Amtrak
Empire Builder
Burlington Northern Santa Fe Railway
Fallbridge Subdivision
April 14, 1999

A rarity for the Portland section of Amtrak's Empire Builder: Two locomotives -- #113 and #803 --
head the short passenger train as it goes east along the Columbia River on its way to Spokane.

◀ "LEANING TO THE WEST"
Burlington Northern Santa Fe Railway
Fallbridge Subdivision
Cooks, Washington
March 10, 1999

BNSF 9-44CW #761 and Santa Fe F45U #5988 pull a westbound stack train toward Vancouver.

"LET US HANDLE IT"
Union Pacific Railroad
Portland Subdivision
The Dalles, Oregon
August 1997

"REGULATOR LINE"
Union Pacific Railroad
Portland Subdivision
The Dalles, Oregon
February 7, 1998

Passing an ancient billboard that advertises steamship service to Portland for $1, UP SD50 #5006 leads a gravel train through The Dalles, Oregon, early in 1998. The Getchell Building, on which the sign is painted, was built in 1863, and is the oldest remaining building in The Dalles. Wheat, livestock, general merchandise, and passengers were transported on the steamships during the 1880s and 1890s, when river service was the "freeway" of its era.

"COFC"
Burlington Northern Santa Fe Railway
Fallbridge Subdivision
MP 82.3
April 22, 1998

BN C30-7 #5071 leads a container train west out of Tunnel #7 on the Fallbridge Subdivision near Lyle, Washington.

Leaving the siding at East Bingen, Washington, a "grain empties" train rumbles east-bound behind five BN locomotives in the carrier's tradi-tional green and white paint scheme. Included in the consist are BN GP40 #3503 up front and two SD9s in fading paint at the rear. Sights like this have suddenly become unusual, as BNSF repaints more locomotives into its orange-flavored merger colors. The nearly solid green train is striking against the foreground of desert parsley, with its bright yellow flowers and light green leaves. The colorful plants bloom all around the Columbia River Gorge in the spring.

"SPRING GREEN"
Burlington Northern Santa Fe Railway
Fallbridge Subdivision
East Bingen, Washington
April 5, 1998

37

"INLAND"
Union Pacific Railroad
Portland Subdivision
Wyeth, Oregon
July 1998

"RUST AND STEEL"
Burlington Northern Santa Fe Railway
Fallbridge Subdivision
Hood, Washington
January 1999

Steel wheels on a string of deadlined Great Northern hoppers gather rust on a siding.

About half an hour after the final westbound Pioneer has cleared, the final eastbound run of The Pioneer passes by on its journey to Chicago. The two Amtrak trains -- both led by a solo F40PH -- passed each other at the nearby Mosier siding, about three miles west of this location.

"LAST EASTBOUND"
Amtrak
The Pioneer
Union Pacific's Portland Subdivision
Rowena, Oregon
May 10, 1997

"SOLO TRY"
Mount Hood Railroad
Odell, Oregon
April 19, 1998

A single Alco C415 (#701) pulls the Mount Hood's dinner train past a new season's blossoms. The "Spirit of Oregon" dinner train -- previously operated on a portion of the Port of Tillamook Bay Railroad's line along the Oregon coast -- arrived in Hood River in mid-March, 1997. The train began service between Hood River and Parkdale in April 1997, behind ex-Columbia & Cowlitz Alcos #701 and #702. By the end of 1998, both the Alcos had been sold, although the dinner train remained in business behind a Mount Hood GP9. The entire train set included four excursion cars: A bar car, (former Alaska Railroad #10); A kitchen car (a former Great Northern 200-series baggage car); and two dining cars (ex-Northern Pacific coaches #505 and #507).

"SPSF CAB"
Santa Fe Railway caboose #999088
Burlington Northern Santa Fe Railway
Fallbridge Subdivision
Bingen, Washington
November 19, 1999

A relic from the proposed Southern Pacific/Santa Fe merger in the 1980s that the ICC rejected, this caboose was reportedly one of only seven Santa Fe cabooses to be painted into the doomed merger's paint scheme. This particular caboose was set out in Bingen on the way to its final resting place on a private buyer's property.

"SILVER LEAVES"
Burlington Northern Santa Fe Railway
Fallbridge Subdivision
Bingen, Washington
August 12, 1999

With the silver undersides of the cottonwood tree leaves shining in the breeze, the Wishram Local -- headed by GP39M #2899 and GP39-2 #2717 -- moves east after completing its daily switching chores between Wishram and Home Valley along Washington's Columbia River.

The daily Wishram Local, headed by GP30 #2745 and GP38-2 #2259, whizzes past signal towers at MP 80.2 on its run toward Home Valley, Washington, with six cars.

"WISHRAM LOCAL"
Burlington Northern Santa Fe Railway
Fallbridge Subdivision
Rowland Lake, Washington
May 28, 1999

With the Columbia River in the background, freshly-painted HLCX #6077 and Soo Line #6613 cross a stone bridge over the mouth of the Klickitat River at Lyle, Washington. The out-of-place pair of SD40-2s are leading an eastbound train of empty grain hoppers along the BNSF mainline between Vancouver and Pasco, Washington.

"KLICKITAT CROSSING"
Burlington Northern Santa Fe Railway
Fallbridge Subdivision
Lyle, Washington
April 18, 1998

"LIGHTNING STRIKE"
Union Pacific Railroad
Portland Subdivision
Rowena, Oregon
September 30, 1998

"ENTER HERE"
Burlington Northern Santa Fe Railway
Fallbridge Subdivision
Cooks, Washington
March 14, 1999

"TUNNEL FACE"
Burlington Northern Railroad
Fallbridge Subdivision
Cooks, Washington
March 27, 1995

A westbound Burlington Northern grain train blasts out of Tunnel #2 near Cooks, Washington, on Burlington Northern's Fallbridge Subdivision mainline. Note how the exhaust from hundreds of trains has blackened the rock face of the rough-hewn tunnel. It is March 1995, and BN is using a mixture of multiple SD40-2s and a cabless B30-7AB to power another long train.

45

"TROUGH TRAIN"
Burlington Northern Santa Fe Railway
Fallbridge Subdivision
North Dalles, Washington
March 11, 1998

One of BNSF's flagship coal trains, led by BNSF SD70MAC #9550, comes west through the Columbia River Gorge. The innovative train is on its way from the Powder River Basin in Wyoming to a power plant at Centralia, Washington. Coal trains run three times a week through the Gorge, but the expensive "trough trains" are rarely seen.

An eastbound rolls past the abandoned Broughton Lumber Company mill at Hood, Washington, on Independence Day, 1998.

"BROUGHTON"
Burlington Northern Santa Fe Railway
Fallbridge Subdivision
Hood, Washington
July 4, 1998

"SEEING DOUBLE"
Union Pacific Railroad
Portland Subdivision
Rowena, Oregon
March 29, 2000

"SOO LINE DREAMS"
Soo Line Railroad
Ashland, Wisconsin
June 23, 1999

Derelict Soo Line signal towers stand, ghostly, as if still protecting the lead to Ashland's once busy ore loading docks. The ore operation on the Lake Superior shore at Ashland has been out of service since the 1960s.

"MONARCH"
South Manitou Island, Michigan
August 1997

II Heartland: Dreams of The Upper Midwest

I was born and raised at the mouth of the Hazzard Holler
Where the coal cars rolled and rumbled past my door
Now they stand in a rusty row of all empties
Because the L&N don't stop here anymore.

— Jean Ritchie, "The L&N Don't Stop Here Anymore," Geordie Music Publishing Co. (ASCAP)

"AT QUITTING TIME"
Tuscola & Saginaw Bay Railway
Cadillac, Michigan
June 28, 1999

It is 5 p.m. on June 28, 1999, and a pair of Tuscola & Saginaw Bay Railway GP35s (#388 and #392) have just pulled up to the engine house in Cadillac, Michigan, after handling switching duties in the industrial part of the city. The two units, in fresh paint, are named "City of Petoskey" and "City of Mt. Pleasant" for key on-line towns. Both are former Ann Arbor Railroad locomotives.

In HEMINGWAY *Country*

In his 1925 short story, "The Battler," Ernest Hemingway wrote about a young character named Nick Adams, a guy who loved the outdoors and seemed to be caught up in his wanderlust.

The setting of this particular tale was northern Michigan, and more specifically, along the Pennsylvania Railroad line that started in Mackinaw City, Michigan, and ran south through Petoskey, Kalkaska, Cadillac, Grand Rapids, and eventually to Fort Wayne, Indiana. The line was built as the Grand Rapids & Indiana, which was absorbed by the Pennsylvania in 1869.

Hemingway's story was fictional, but the towns and trains he wrote about were real. As "The Battler" begins, Nick has just been tossed off a through freight by a crusty brakeman who didn't want him riding his train.

Hemingway described how Nick had swung on to the northbound freight as it "slowed down for the yards outside of Walton Junction," then rode on "through Kalkaska as it started to get dark."

The train was nearing Mancelona when Nick was discovered by the no-nonsense brakeman, and a moment later, Nick watched from the roadbed cinders as the lights of the caboose disappeared around a curve.

Dazed and feeling his bruises, he stumbled into a hobo camp where an old, ex-prizefighter (hence the name of the story) and his friend were cooking up dinner over an open fire.

In a way, Hemingway's well-chosen title transcends what he describes in the story. In a fashion Hemingway couldn't have foreseen in the 1920s when he produced the manuscript, the railroad line itself -- by surviving in the late-1990s -- has proven to be a true battler, like the aging fighter in his narrative.

In the years following Hemingway's death in 1961, the route cutting north-south through Michigan has been operated by four different owners, including two Class I carriers -- the Pennsylvania and Penn Central; and two shortlines -- Michigan Northern Railway and the Tuscola & Saginaw Bay Railway.

I first read "The Battler" in a college literature class in 1972. Even then, the future of the line was in jeopardy. Penn Central had inherited the property, and the carrier, faced with financial problems everywhere, didn't put a lot of energy into improving service along the line. A local based out of Cadillac occasionally roamed north and south; through freights and passenger trains were gone.

To no one's surprise, the line wasn't included in the Conrail reorganization of 1976, so in April of that year, Michigan Northern took over operations between Comstock Park (just north of Grand Rapids) and Mackinaw City. Michigan Northern gave it a good fight for a few years, but succumbed when it lost its connection to the north with Soo Line via the carferry *Chief Wawatam*, which ran across the Straits of Mackinac to link the shortline with a Soo Line terminal in St. Ignace.

In the late 1990s, not much of Pennsylvania's ex-GR&I Branch -- now operated by the Tuscola & Saginaw Bay Railroad -- remains intact. The Grand Rapids to Cadillac segment has been abandoned, and the track between Petoskey and Mackinaw City is gone as well. But between Cadillac and Petoskey, where approximately 92 miles of ex-Pennsylvania rails remain, trains continue to roll faithfully: The shortline hauls freight to and from Petoskey two to three days a week as needed, and heads into Traverse City, via Walton Junction, three to four days a week.

Hemingway, I believe, would be pleased.

"ANN ARBOR MEMORIES"
Tuscola & Saginaw Bay Railroad
Ann Arbor Railroad #74
Cadillac, Michigan
June 28, 1999

With its flag logo still relatively sharp, an ex-Ann Arbor Railroad cement hopper, AA #74, rests ignored in a desolate Tuscola & Saginaw Bay Railroad freight yard in Cadillac, Michigan. When the AARR was active, Cadillac was an important station on the north-south line that linked the carferry docks at Elberta, Michigan, with Toledo, Ohio.

FREE RIVER

There was something special about the wood of Kelly's home. Rough against my palm and threatening slivers, still it felt good.

How many more hours?

The entire place felt good. I stood there leaning against the weathered wall facing the Platte River and listened to the hypnotic sounds of the northern Michigan forest. And listened for the arrival of Kelly.

Oh God. It was supposed to be another last night in yet another town. Supposed to be. The "last night" part of it was my idea, like everything else lately, but I was starting to wonder about leaving this time.

Why?

I was solitary in Kelly's isolated cabin for a while. She was away, in Traverse City for some everyday type of errands, the kind I'd almost forgotten about. Four months of drifting town-to-town can make you forget about things like that. About a lot of things. I heard Kelly's van through the trees, heard it slipping up the sand and gravel roadway toward her property. I was surprised to feel my heart suddenly accelerating.

She came out back to join me close to where the river was hissing alongside the sandy bank, and we held each other like longtime lovers.

Inside the house, music from Bob Dylan's *Blood On the Tracks* album played. Haunting lyrics drifted out from her warm dwelling, reached Kelly and I, and bounced around off aspen leaves and slender tree trunks:

"... And I've never gotten used to it, I've just learned to turn it off; either I'm too sensitive, or else I'm getting soft. Sundown, yellow moon, I replay the past. I know every scene by heart, they all went by so fast..."

It had rained earlier. The sky was an eerie glow, a storm-pale yellow against the light forest green. Kelly stood out there in the strange lighting, all misty and ghostly, then began spinning around joyfully.

I couldn't take my eyes off her.

I began to feel more involvement with Kelly, with her home and her life. It made no sense; 10 days ago I'd never seen her face or uttered a phrase to her. Yet now it was beginning to grow tempting to think of staying with her, in the solid cabin and among the lush surroundings with the free river flowing past. She'd made it clear that I was absolutely welcome to stay.

That made me sad.

In her bed that night, there was an unreal

edge to our communication.

"I'd better leave before I get too involved," I told her, as if to reveal my uncertainty about what we were doing together. Maybe she would say something that could dispel the obscurity; something that would make me see sharply: stay here, or move on.

"It's so hard to talk to you, the things you say are so vague," she responded. Then, a moment later: "Just kiss me."

And for a time, at least, kissing felt like enough.

In the darkness of early morning she slid over me, seeming hungry, an ungentle passion between us racing to be met. It seemed as if we were trying to deny that our parting scene was looming so near by remaining physically joined. Perhaps we could thus cheat inevitability in some mystical way.

The next day, I caught myself looking at the clock while making love with her, checking the time; attempting to figure how many more hours we'd have if I rearranged my plans, if I left on this day instead of that, at this hour instead of that. And I understood finally how cruelly the cards could be dealt. For both of us, I knew I had to get out of there. There was a reckoning. It couldn't be ignored, or delayed any longer.

Kelly offered to drive me to Clare, a rough quar-ter of the distance to Jackson, my latest destination. It was a final gift of opportunity -- to be together, and possibly to change our world.

Along the way, she drove us through some tree-lined, romantic back lane she liked, and my hands were all over her. She responded to my touch with her one free hand, and I nuzzled closer. Being with her felt sweet. I didn't want it to end.

"Why don't you just quit," I said.

For a moment, she believed I was telling her to leave me alone, asking her not to touch me.

"I mean your job," I added.

"Well, I never know about you," she laughed, then waited, open, for me to elaborate.

But it became a notion only, and at nearly the same time I offered the words I faced a different vision: finding myself craving new sights, and no confinements. The call was too strong. Even as I discovered just how much I longed to stay with Kelly, too strong.

There was no magical way around the tangle, and I figured Kelly would understand.

At the appointed spot, she stopped her van.

I left her in Clare, the junction of Highway 10 eastbound with Highway 27 southbound; the junction of the Ann Arbor Railroad with the Chesapeake & Ohio.

"WAITING ROOM"

Escanaba & Lake Superior Railroad
Sidnaw, Michigan
June 23, 1999

*During a hard June rain in Sidnaw, Michigan, an old shanty looms out of the trackside mist with a humble
bench and a station sign that seems more impressive than the building it is attached to. Mainlines of the Soo
Line and the Milwaukee Road once crossed here, but the Soo Line track to the west is long gone, while the
Escanaba & Lake Superior Railroad operates the former Milwaukee Road line northwest to Ontonagon.*

"THE MASTER TRACK"
Minnesota Commercial Railroad
St. Paul, Minnesota
June 21, 1999

Let the time blast through like a moving train, because there's no time to wonder if you're doing the right thing when you're grabbing a rolling train — you just wake up in Toronto.

— Scott A. Sparling, Seattle, Washington, March 20, 1984

'61 VALIANT

You can't watch a train from inside your car. You can, of course. But the essence of train is lost. Step outside and the music of the train starts thumping against your chest, and you feel more alive.

One sunny morning in Minneapolis, near Lake Street where the Burlington Northern tracks run, I was sitting in my 1961 Valiant eating a blintz when an eastbound came snaking along from the yards beyond Cedar Lake ... a long slow freight headed toward St. Paul and, from there, beyond. It was a Friday in July 1976, and I had taken a day off work, and eating the blintz was my only plan.

With nothing particular in mind, I got out of my car, simply so I could hear the train better. While I was standing there, it stopped. It would have been easy to climb on at that point, though I had no plans to do so.

The tracks run through that part of the city in a gully, going east-west. Passing time, I walked to the nearest north-south street, which formed an overpass over the train, and stood there looking down at it.

When the train started to move, I thought how easy it would be to jump down from the overpass onto the top of a boxcar, as you might see in a movie.

It could even be done holding a blintz, I thought. But I quickly finished the blintz -- so I'd have both hands free, just in case.

Instead of a boxcar, I chose an empty auto rack. The train was picking up speed, so I had to anticipate a little ... jump a second ahead of my target so I didn't miss the rack and fall between cars. And of course, stay down once I landed, so as not to be brained by the overpass.

I was 22 at the time. I'm 44 now. I don't jump from overpasses any more, but I did that day, and I remember it being easier than I thought it was going to be. I landed close to prone, with my arms cushioning the fall, as if I was finishing a push-up. Then I simply rolled over and lay there on my back while Minneapolis rolled gracefully by. The sky was a deep blue. I was proud of myself.

I rolled across the Mississippi River on that auto rack. Trains being what they are, it took about four hours to get from the western edge of Minneapolis to Pig's Eye Yard in St. Paul. But I was in no hurry. I dozed. I got a little sunburned.

In those days, and nights, I would occasionally walk out on the railroad bridge that crossed the Mississippi, climb up on the short sidewall and stand there with my toes to the edge, the wind at my back -- innocently checking to see if my destiny included being blown off the bridge. It wasn't the normal sort of thing to do, and I don't recommend it, though it felt normal at the time. It wasn't any kind of daredevil-suicide flirtation thing. It just made me feel alive, like listening to good music. Once, I went out there with my girlfriend and I was surprised to learn that she didn't appreciate the experience. Wouldn't anyone like the chance to feel the world right there in the wind, in the night? Like the Bob Seger lyric that hadn't yet been written: *"I took my young son/to the river/I put his hand out/to feel the rain."*

I was too young at the time to appreciate the danger, or maybe now I'm just too old. Regardless ... I had always hoped to ride across that bridge on a freight, having stood there many a night.

And so, because I happened to get out of my car -- all to hear the train a little better -- I happened to stand on the overpass ... and my hope came true.

I'm not saying this will happen to you if you get out of your car next time you see a train. But I am saying, there's more life out there than you can see through any windshield.

— Scott A. Sparling, Lake Oswego, Oregon, October 1997

"MANITOWOC FOG"
Fox Valley & Western Railroad
Manitowoc District
Manitowoc, Wisconsin
August 1997

A lone seagull perches on the railing of the long Fox Valley & Western Railroad bridge heading south across the Manitowoc River. The bumpy tracks, formerly owned by Chicago & NorthWestern, cut north-south from Manitowoc on a moribund route from Manitowoc to Sheboygan, Wisconsin, a remnant of what was once a key C&NW trunk route between Milwaukee and Green Bay. The "no trespassing" sign on the bridge is still lettered for Fox Valley & Western predecessor Fox River Valley Railroad. FV&W purchased both the Fox River Valley and the Green Bay & Western Railroad in August 1993; the 507-mile FV&W system was later absorbed into Midwest regional Wisconsin Central Railroad.

Behind GP35 #2060, WC's Munising Local is pulling out of Munising Junction, Michigan, with eight cars in tow, headed east on the return half of its tri-weekly round trip from Trout Lake.

"MUNISING TO TROUT LAKE"
Wisconsin Central Railroad
Munising Junction, Michigan
June 24, 1999

"LONG VIEW"
Wisconsin Central Railroad
Munising Junction, Michigan
June 24, 1999

The ex-Soo Line Railroad's main track to Marquette, seen at Munising Junction, Michigan. This view looks west toward Marquette. A section of rail has been removed, with formal abandonment apparently looming. Marquette, one of the larger cities in Michigan's Upper Peninsula and once a key station for the Soo Line, lost importance following the decline of taconite ore traffic. The ore loading docks on Marquette's waterfront have been abandoned.

"MICHIGAN HAULER"
Wisconsin Central Railroad
Manistique, Michigan
June 30, 1999

WC's key east-west hauler in the Upper Peninsula of Michigan is the daily through freight between Sault Ste. Marie, Ontario, and Gladstone, Michigan. Headed westbound near Manistique, Michigan, on June 30, 1999, the train is pulled by a consist that includes WC SD45 #7495, colorful Algoma Central F-unit #1753, and WC GP40 #3005.

"ONE LINE REMAINS"
Wisconsin Central Railroad
Ashland, Wisconsin
June 23, 1999

Ex-Soo Line GP30 #719 and Wisconsin Central GP35 #2555 lead the daily freight north into Ashland, Wisconsin, at 9 a.m. on a wet June day in 1999. Ashland was once served by three railroads -- Chicago & NorthWestern, Soo Line, and Burlington Northern -- but now only WC remains to serve the northern Wisconsin town. In the 1970s, lines radiated out of Ashland in four directions, but now only a southbound line (to Mellen, Wisconsin) remains in service. A close look at the front of #719 reveals that an effort was made to paint over a portion of the old locomotive's former Soo Line identity.

"REST IN PEACE"
Bangor & Aroostook Railroad
GP7 #66
St. Paul, Minnesota
June 1999

"BOAT TRACKS"
Fox Valley & Western Railroad
Kewaunee Subdivision
Kewaunee, Wisconsin
August 1997

The view at MP 30.3, facing east along ex-Green Bay & Western rails leading into Kewaunee, Wisconsin, in August 1997. Until the 1980s, these tracks hosted the daily GB&W "boat trains" from Green Bay, which served the railroad carferries that crossed Lake Michigan. Bound from Kewaunee to Frankfort and Ludington, Michigan, the carferries provided a rail connection with the Ann Arbor Railroad and the Chessie System, respectively. In 1997, with the ferries long gone and freight service to Kewaunee virtually non-existent, this line segment is lucky to have survived. But its days are dwindling: In January 1998, new owner Fox Valley & Western Railroad filed an abandonment petition that would lead to the removal of much of the line linking Green Bay and Kewaunee. The carrier wants to drop 17 miles of track, from Kewaunee (MP 35.6) to Luxemburg (MP 18.9). The wooden milepost marker, with the specific location in black paint, recalls a different era.

"LUCKY AT CAMERON"
Wisconsin Central Railroad
Cameron, Wisconsin
June 21, 1999

Nearing Cameron, Wisconsin, Wisconsin Central's weekday Ladysmith-Almena local comes east to a crossing with a once-busy former Chicago & NorthWestern route between Eau Claire, Wisconsin, and Duluth, Minnesota. The old C&NW line now terminates at Rice Lake, about seven miles north of the Cameron diamond. WC GP35 #2553 is pulling this day's cut of about 10 cars. Note the swinging metal gate on the right; a stop sign on the gate protects the WC line from north-south traffic.

"LAST ORDER"
Molalla Western Railroad
Molalla Branch
Liberal, Oregon
August 1996

Photo by Deborah A. Winter

New SP boxcars, in storage near Liberal, Oregon, were part of SP's final order for new freight cars before the September 1996 merger with Union Pacific. The boxcars, built in nearby Portland by freight car builder Gunderson, Inc., were temporarily stored on the out-of-service southern segment of shortline Molalla Western's 10 miles of track between Canby and Molalla.

"STOP SIGN"
Union Pacific Railroad
Condon Branch
Gilliam, Oregon
February 9, 1997

III The West Coast:
Rolling Images

" *If love was a train, I think I would ride me a long one*
Hear me talking -- 50 boxcars long …
Aw, what's the use?
Most trains these days ain't got no engine,
Much less a caboose. "

— Michelle Shocked, "If Love Was A Train," PolyGram Songs, Inc. (BMI)

"BICENTENNIAL"
Western Pacific Railroad
Oroville Line
Paxton, California
July 28, 1978

Photo by Don Flynn

Shelter

We split up in Klamath Falls,
to seek empties;
each taking a direction
on that long long string of mostly sealed freight.
It was one north, one south
into the darkness, the distance,
the biting autumn air …
Wondering if we would somehow find an open car;
Wondering if we would somehow become separated
in the blackness and expanse of nighttime yard.

All for the Feather River reward:
On our way to icy Twain,
and to sleep on frosty flats;
We opened shiny new Mississippi Export boxcars
to get the paint smell out of them.

"INDUSTRIAL STRENGTH"
Southern Pacific Railroad
SD9 #4346
Valley Line
Millersburg, Oregon
April 3, 1990

Southern Pacific's Valley Line in Oregon is the mainline route between Portland and Eugene, and normally sees long freights and daily Amtrak runs. On April 3, 1990, SP SD9 #4346 is all by itself, running south toward Albany after switching an industrial area in nearby Millersburg. The locomotive's heavy-duty service shows on its finish, with #4346 appearing to be in need of a good washing and a new coat of paint.

"Yes I had a woman love me
I gave her what there was of me
And it was good, as it could be
Then I heard a wild world calling
I saw a lone star falling
I caught a song and set it free."

— Rodney Crowell, "Many A Long and Lonesome Highway," Coolwell Music (ASCAP)

VISIONS *of* Responsibility

What direction is my life taking? North.
Then east.
North by northeast.
"Well, I guess I'm packed and ready," I said
vaguely, to the empty room. My voice came
back unfamiliar.
Go. Go on. Go ahead then.
"Farewell."

—Journal entry, Corvallis, Oregon, May 1979

May was almost gone, and so was my time in Corvallis. I'd only been there a few months, since December, but it had run its course. Six months and I was restless already.

Outside, a soft rain was falling. It coated the windows and obscured a moonlight view of silhouetted Coast Range hills. Inside, a lone candle burned brightly in my upstairs room. I was sitting on my mat, bolt upright at 3 a.m., studying maps displaying the West Coast, from Alaska to Baja. But my eyes kept returning to a photograph of Marie that tried to sit unobtrusively on a corner table.

I drifted into sleep and dreams crowded in on me. Then suddenly I was awake, recalling Marie next to me in the hills above Ashland, Oregon: her hands on me, the energy of our connection. She wasn't meeting with me in the hills any longer. And Ashland seemed far too distant.

Marie had been my sweetheart; I'd met her when she was all of 17 (and I was all of 20) in Ann Arbor, Michigan, one summer day. We were pretty much inseparable from that point on -- for a few years, anyway.

We moved west together; discovered Ashland in 1975 and lived contentedly in that peaceful and magical town for two years. During that period I thought I had everything, but vulnerability to wanderlust and an unexpected passion for another woman got the better of me and on an April morning I left it all behind.

For five months I toured the North American

continent in pursuit of siren Brenda, shouldered with a romantic, gypsy lust to be with her. I met up with her in Canton, Ohio, in a hard rain. I stared into her deep blue eyes and she stared right back, and the world felt magical and right.

But after a few sweet weeks with Brenda a fresh restlessness overruled my heart, and I said goodbye to her at the Conrail freight yard in Crestline.

Sweeping as far to the east as the continent would allow, I traveled to Halifax, Nova Scotia; distant from any hint of commitment to either woman, and gazed out over an endless ocean.

In September, I finally wound my way back to Oregon and to Marie. She seemed torn between joy at my return and anger at my long absence and the unhidden reasons I'd been away, and I learned what it felt like to witness something precious being shattered.

Ashland and the contentment I'd felt there became history. Marie and I stayed in contact, but gravitated to separate towns. We visited each other now and then, and remained lovers, but if we had a partnership it was a partnership in limbo. Our relationship, perhaps, could best be described as hopeful chaos, or maybe passionate chaos. And after five years of involvement, I didn't know where, or whether, our relationship was going -- except deeper into confusion.

In Vancouver, British Columbia, on the way back from a short vacation together on Alaska's Revillagigedo Island, I once again said farewell to Marie. She had to get back to her job in Eugene, while I planned further travel; there were no limits on my time. The U.S. Forest Service job I'd held in the Siuslaw National Forest had ended the previous December, and part-time work I'd entertained since then in Corvallis had dried up. I faced no deadlines and no pressing responsibilities; simply, I'd return to Oregon when I felt like it. I still didn't understand there might be a price to pay for my recklessness; the future seemed only promising.

Marie and I stood close on the platform at the Vancouver railway station until she had to board the VIA passenger train to go south. When the train pulled away, it was tough to take the sight of her hand raised and her dark eyes directly fixed upon me, silently imploring me not to stay away too long.

Later that day, I grabbed an eastward passenger train out of Vancouver. Reaching Moose Jaw, Saskatchewan, one night, I left VIA and sat in a grassy field beside Canadian Pacific Railway tracks, mulling the mysteries of life.

There were no immediate answers.

At the end of the breakwater at Frankfort, Michigan, I sat quietly under the revolving beam of a Coast Guard lighthouse that marked the entrance to Betsie Bay. While I watched, a cluster of lights on the horizon drew closer and turned into the Ann Arbor Railroad's carferry *The City of Milwaukee*, coming toward Frankfort from the west, across Lake Michigan. As the waves generated by the twin-funneled carferry's passage slapped against the cement jetty, I longed to be heading back that way. At last I was feeling solid, ready to return; maybe even ready to settle.

I journeyed westward hopefully, although my pace was meanderingly slow. I looked forward to reaching Oregon again, and warmly anticipated wrapping myself in Marie's affectionate arms. I believed we could work everything out, and finally create long-term plans together. I craved that.

I rode a nighttime Rock Island Railroad freight south from Owatonna, Minnesota, and left the train in Mason City, Iowa, when it paused at a crossing with the Milwaukee Road's east-west mainline.

The next morning I met Jean. I'd asked her for directions to a coin laundry, and later she came there looking for me. Warm and gentle, she wanted me to stay with her in Mason City for a day, a night, a week. There was a spark of desire glowing between us, and I knew again of my vulnerability. But I yielded faithful to Marie and my new visions of responsibility, and left Jean untouched.

I had rolled west out of Michigan on July 20. Ten

days later, I had made it only as far west as Montevideo, Minnesota. Ten days! At that rate it would have taken another month to reach Oregon.

From Montevideo, stuck in one-train-a-day territory and waiting for a westbound freight out of distant St. Paul, I called Marie. She sounded tentative and uncharacteristically cold over the telephone.

"Where are you?" she asked.

I told her.

She responded, as if accusing: "You're only in Minnesota and you left Michigan on July 20th?"

Pointing out that Montevideo was in *western* Minnesota seemed weak and insignificant, so I didn't bother. Maybe she thought the next time she heard from me I'd be into Idaho -- or somewhere a lot closer than Minnesota, at least. Maybe she feared the presence of another woman. Maybe she needed more than a fleeting, wire-distant voice; more than flat words on mailed pieces of paper that by their very nature could offer no more than unstated promise.

The exact reasons didn't really matter, I suppose. What mattered was her pain, and I felt it. The gulf between us was great, and standing in a dreary phone booth in Minnesota, I was powerless to dispel it. Worse, all the spirited affection I'd been wanting to share -- the sensuality of crossing the land bound for her -- I found I couldn't convey.

I reached Missoula, Montana, on one of the last transcontinental trains operated by the Milwaukee Road -- a carrier that was slipping into bankruptcy and would not be crossing the land much longer. Traveling felt soulful and poetic.

I stayed in the Palace Hotel in downtown Missoula, Room 404. From there, I again telephoned Marie. She sounded caring, and everything felt fine. I still couldn't give her the exact date that I'd reach her, but at least she knew I was closing in.

When I got back to Eugene a few days later, I discovered Marie in the darkened apartment of a neighbor, drink in hand. Just the two of them. She seemed surprised to see me. She paused in the shadow of the guy's dim doorway, as if once again unsure whether she was happy to see me or in resentment at my delayed return; as if confused about whether she wanted to step forward or back.

And if she didn't know, it wasn't going to work.

Maybe I could have stayed, tried to make some sense out of it with her, but our relationship had become an unyielding, tangled thread. The passage of time, instead of making anything clearer, had only widened the gap between the course of our lives. There had been too much distance, too many opportunities forsaken. Ultimately, that had wedged us apart.

The time in limbo I put behind me. In 1982 I moved to Arizona, living in a desert ranchhouse 25 miles out of Tucson and less than 30 miles from the Mexican border.

At night I sat on my flat pebbled roof and thought about Ashland; about Revillagigedo Island; about Mason City; about unsigned forks in the road.

One day a friend wrote, and mentioned he'd heard that Marie had married -- apparently not the neighbor at least -- and they'd moved to Spokane.

I felt settled.

"MITSUI O.S.K."
Mitsui O.S.K. Lines
Forest Grove, Oregon
September 1993

The wonderful "alligator carrying a trunk" logo has been common on trailers and containers traveling North American railroads since the 1970s. But its history goes back a lot further than that: the Japanese transportation company, based in Tokyo, has been moving goods since 1884, when it originated as the Mitsui Steamship Company. The "O.S.K." was added in 1964, following a merger with Osaka Shosen Kaisha Line. Mitsui O.S.K.'s operations include land, air, and sea transportation on a worldwide scale.

"BLACK WIDOW"
Willamette & Pacific Railroad
GP9 #1801
Bailey District
Dawson, Oregon
April 13, 1995

Willamette & Pacific's Dawson Local switches the Hull-Oakes mill, at the end of what used to be Southern Pacific's Bailey Branch, in April 1995. W&P's clean locomotive is a GP9, built in 1959 and repainted in the old Southern Pacific "Black Widow" colors in 1994.

◀ **"LUMBER FROM OREGON"**
Southern Pacific Railroad
Bailey Branch
Dawson, Oregon
November 8, 1990

Southern Pacific's Dawson Local, returning to Corvallis, Oregon, with loads of lumber, rolls eastward past MP 679, just out of Dawson. The milepost marker signifies that the train is 679 miles by rail from SP's traditional headquarters in San Francisco.

73

"MERGER TRICKS"
Union Pacific Railroad
Canyon Subdivision
Quincy Junction, California
May 27, 1996

It looks a lot like the scenery in the Midwest, maybe Wisconsin, or perhaps the Mississippi River country around the Iowa/Illinois border somewhere. The Chicago & NorthWestern units, along with the cargo of automobiles, reinforce that impression. But actually, it's not a C&NW line through the Midwest. Rather, it is Union Pacific's northern California mainline between Portola and Oakland, California, caught at Quincy Junction at 10 a.m. on May 27, 1996. The train is westbound behind two C&NW locomotives: C40-8 #8704 and SD60 #8033.

"POWER MIX"
Southern Pacific Railroad
Coast Line
San Luis Obispo, California
September 30, 1995

Sleek new Amtrak power heads the northbound Coast Starlight as it rolls up alongside heavy SP road units (SD40-2 #7359 & SD40T-2 #8262) in Southern Pacific's freight yard in sunny San Luis Obispo, California, in the autumn of 1995.

"CORVALLIS JUNCTION"
Southern Pacific Railroad
Dallas Local
Corvallis Junction, Oregon
April 11, 1990

The Dallas Local returns to Corvallis Junction, where the Toledo Branch and the West Side Branch join, on its way to the crew's home base in Corvallis. The local train, running three times a week in the early 1990s, ventures about 25 miles to the north to serve customers along the West Side Branch and the Dallas Branch. On this day, SD9 #4411 provided all the power the short train required.

"REEDSPORT"
Southern Pacific Railroad
Coos Bay Line
Reedsport, Oregon
July 26, 1993

Southern Pacific's Coos Bay Hauler rolls north through the rich Coast Range foothills into Reedsport, Oregon, in July 1993. The freight is headed to Eugene, with three of SP's once-ubiquitous SD9s (#4410, #4301, and #4377) doing the hauling.

75

"STENCIL IDENTITY"
Willamette & Pacific Railroad
SD9 #1852
West Side District
McMinnville, Oregon
August 1996

Willamette & Pacific Railroad SD9 #1852 rests between switching assignments in the McMinnville yard. Although the W&P logo has been stenciled on, the unit retains the basic paint scheme of its former owner, Southern Pacific. McMinnville is one of W&P's key bases, where several locomotives are often idling.

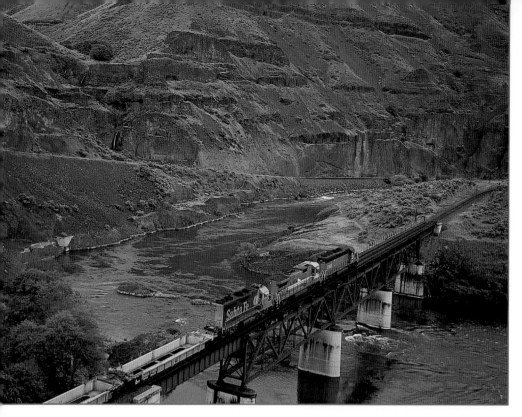

"RIVER CANYON"
Burlington Northern Santa Fe Railway
Oregon Trunk Subdivision
Sherar, Oregon
May 28, 1997

Crossing a bridge over the Deschutes River, three mixed locomotives move a trainload of empty container cars south on the Oregon Trunk in May 1997. Pulling are BN SD40-2 #7158, LMX B39-8 #8562, and Santa Fe GP35 #2920.

Virtually all freight trains on Burlington Northern Santa Fe's Oregon Trunk Line between Wishram, Washington, and Bend, Oregon, required the use of cabooses into the late 1990s. In May 1997, three cabooses -- BN #12030, BN #12207, and BN #12188 -- are rolling north through Moody, Oregon, on the rear of a long mixed merchandise train bound for Wishram, Washington.

"BRING EXTRA"
Burlington Northern Santa Fe Railway
Oregon Trunk Subdivision
Moody, Oregon
May 23, 1997

77

"AT THE SUMMIT"
Central Oregon & Pacific Railroad
Siskiyou Line
Siskiyou Summit, Oregon
May 29, 1996

Central Oregon & Pacific Railroad's southbound Montague Hauler arrives at Siskiyou Summit (MP 412.2) in the Siskiyou Mountains of Oregon. As is typical of regional railroads and short-lines in the Northwest, the CO&P employs a mixed heritage of locomotives, thus providing some interesting color schemes. Up front on this train, for example, are six units: ex-Burlington Northern GP40 #3076, ex-Burlington Northern GP40 #3079, ex-Norfolk Southern GP40 #1338, CO&P GP38 #5533, ex-Norfolk Southern GP40 #1335, and CO&P GP38 #5528. Central Oregon & Pacific, based in Roseburg, Oregon, took over a total of about 440 miles of former Southern Pacific lines in Oregon (the Coos Bay Line and the Siskiyou Line) on December 31, 1994. Six months later, CO&P reopened the Siskiyou Line's through route connecting Ashland, Oregon, with Montague, California, which had been taken out of service by SP in August 1992. The California border is only a few miles south of this location.

"LUMBER SWITCH"
Central Oregon & Pacific Railroad
Siskiyou Line
Winchester, Oregon
May 29, 1996

At 5:15 p.m., a northbound Central Oregon & Pacific local headed by lone GP38 #5042 works at Winchester, Oregon. The crew is spotting a cut of RailBox boxcars for one of the area's many trackside lumber mills. Winchester is located at MP 577.8 on the former Southern Pacific Siskiyou Line, which CO&P purchased on the last day of 1994. At this stop, two empty boxcars will be left and one loaded car picked up.

"MORNING CROSSING THE RIVER"
Central Oregon & Pacific Railroad
Coos Bay Line
Reedsport, Oregon
June 16, 1998

CO&P's morning southbound local comes across the Reedsport Drawbridge on its way to Coos Bay in June 1998. The drawbridge crosses the Umpqua River.

"CONSECUTIVE SET"
Southern Pacific Railroad
Valley Line
Halsey, Oregon
June 1989

A northbound mixed freight stretches out behind three freshly refurbished SD45T-2Rs, with the first two units -- Cotton Belt #6869 and Southern Pacific #6868 -- numbered consecutively. The train is racing along Southern Pacific's Valley Line near Halsey, Oregon, en route to Portland's Brooklyn Yard, at the northern end of SP's famed "Golden Empire."

In May 1996 -- only weeks before the final approval of Union Pacific's plans to absorb Southern Pacific Railroad -- two new high-tech locomotives, SP AC4400CWs #375 and #328, pull a long freight westbound on the mountain grade above Truckee, California. Within a few months of when this scene was recorded, Union Pacific locomotives would begin to supplant SP colors, as the new owner moved to blot out the name and corporate image of its long-time rival. Although summer is less than one month away, fresh snow has recently fallen in this part of the Sierra Mountains.

"SOUTHERN PACIFIC TWILIGHT"
Southern Pacific Railroad
Roseville Subdivision
Truckee, California
May 26, 1996

"DREAM OVER"
Southern Pacific Railroad
Mill City Branch
Mill City, Oregon
June 1989

End of the grand transcontinental dreams of Colonel Thomas Egerton Hogg's Oregon Pacific Railroad. At Mill City, Oregon, the tracks come to an inglorious dead end in sight of snow-capped, 10,495-foot Mount Jefferson in the Cascade Range. In 1893, the mountain range looming in the distance proved to be too large an obstacle for the cash-starved Oregon Pacific Railroad to overcome, and the carrier went bankrupt. Southern Pacific later stepped in and ran the line as a branch out of its freight yard in Albany. Had events unfolded differently for the OPRR, however, long-haul freights bound for Boise, Idaho, might still be blazing along this rusting track. Instead, the "Webfoot Route" -- that began near the Pacific Ocean at Yaquina City, Oregon -- hosted only an occasional local serving Mill City Branch lumber mills through the late 1980s and early 1990s. In 1993, a full century after the Oregon Pacific Railroad went bankrupt, owner Southern Pacific leased the line to the Willamette Valley Railroad as part of SP's systemwide effort to streamline its operations to primarily mainline routes.

"DESERT SCRUB"
Union Pacific Railroad
Los Angeles Subdivision
Daggett, California
August 21, 1997

At 6:30 a.m., the desert sun comes up on a "merger team" of C&NW C44-9W #8655 and SP SD40E #7319, pulling a mixed freight slowly westward through Mojave Desert scrub brush at Daggett, California. At Daggett, UP's line from Las Vegas, Nevada, joins with the BNSF Needles Subdivision (Barstow-Needles). UP trains on the Los Angeles Sub operate on BNSF trackage between Daggett and West Riverside, a distance of approximately 102 miles.

Framed by the iron-work of a bridge over multiple yard tracks at Barstow, California, Santa Fe SD39 #1575 and a slug works a cut of cars. Just a month earlier, Santa Fe's merger with Burlington Northern became official.

"YARD WORK"
Burlington Northern Santa Fe Railway
Cajon Subdivision
Barstow, California
September 28, 1995

"IN THE SHADOW OF SP"
Union Pacific Railroad
Valley Subdivision
Dunsmuir, California
August 2, 2000

Behind Southern Pacific C44-9W #8200, a southbound freight leaves Dunsmuir, California, a busy crew change station for UP's north-south trains. Dunsmuir, where UP's Shasta Sub and Valley Sub join, is a famous Western railroad town. It was Southern Pacific property until UP took over in 1996.

"SOUTHBOUND"
Southern Pacific Railroad
Siskiyou Subdivision
Goshen, Oregon
May 1989

Southern Pacific's Yoncalla Local splits the semaphore signal towers as it cuts south near Goshen, Oregon, in May 1989. SD9 #4330 leads a sister SD9 and a long cut of empties for forest products customers along the Siskiyou Line.

"ANTIQUES"
Central Oregon & Pacific Railroad
Roseburg Subdivision
Goshen, Oregon
October 17, 1998

Union Switch & Signal semaphore signal towers shine in the sun just south of Goshen, Oregon, on the Roseburg Sub of Central Oregon & Pacific's Siskiyou Line. The signals remain in use and have been relatively well maintained, although the carrier -- like former owner Southern Pacific before it -- has been seeking permission to remove the antiquated system.

"SHADES OF GREEN"
Burlington Northern Railroad
GP9 #1741
Santiam Branch
Foster, Oregon
March 27, 1991

BN's Santiam Branch Local -- also known as the BN Logger -- leaves Foster, Oregon, after switching a Willamette Industries sawmill at the end of the Santiam Branch. Handling the short train is BN GP9 #1741, built by EMD in the mid-1950s, well over a decade before the corporate entity known as Burlington Northern came into existence. BN's backwater branchlines became some of the last havens for these aging locomotives. Note the contrast between the rusted and scarred GP9 and shiny new BN boxcar #376874, directly behind the engine.

"SHASTA ROUTE"
McCloud Railway
Mount Shasta Line
Mount Shasta, California
August 3, 2000

"WILLAMETTE VALLEY"
Willamette Valley Railroad
GP35 #2502
West Stayton District
Woodburn, Oregon
August 6, 2000

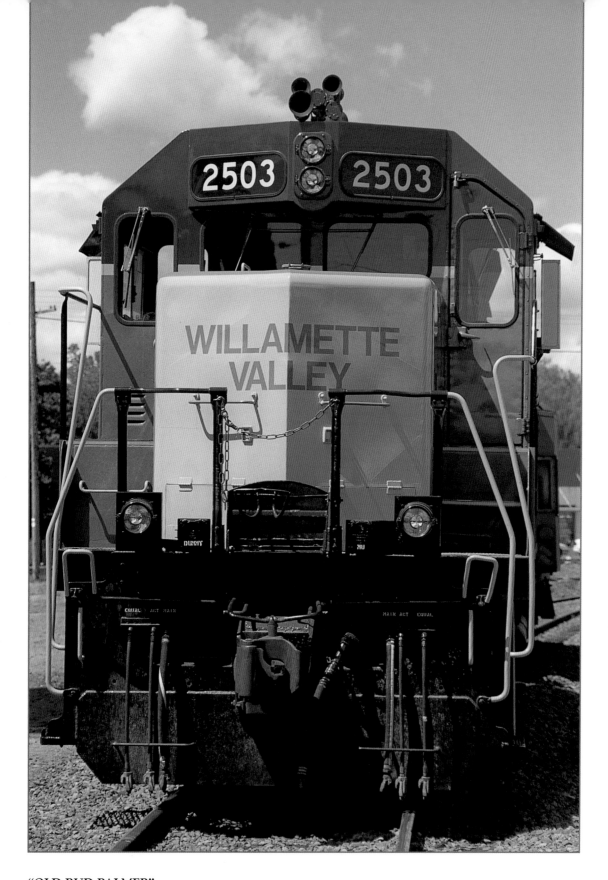

"OLD BUD PALMER"
Willamette Valley Railroad
GP35 #2503
West Stayton District
Woodburn, Oregon
July 19, 1998

Chemult, Oregon, is where the Union Pacific Cascade Line and the BNSF Oregon Trunk Subdivision diverge. Coming north, this BNSF mixed merchandise train cuts off from the UP mainline -- over which it operates via trackage rights -- and onto BNSF rails that will guide the train to Wishram, Washington. BN road power mainstay SD40-2 #7848 is leading a total of four locomotives in the 1970s-era "Barbasol green" paint scheme.

"DIVERTING AT CHEMULT"
Burlington Northern Santa Fe Railway
Oregon Trunk Subdivision
Chemult, Oregon
June 13, 1998

**"LEAVING THE JUNCTION,
FIVE EMPTIES"**
Yreka Western Railroad
Montague, California
June 15, 1998

Yreka Western SW8 #21 slowly moves five empty Southern Pacific woodchip cars west from Montague, California, toward a lumber mill in Yreka. Montague is where the nine-mile Yreka Western Railroad connects with regional carrier Central Oregon & Pacific, operator of the former SP Siskiyou Line.

"AMBROSE SIDING"
Union Pacific Railroad
Modoc Line
Ambrose, California
June 1998

Looking north along the threatened Modoc Line. As part of its overall merger scenario, Union Pacific planned to tear out this segment of former Southern Pacific trackage, which offers an alternative north-south route between Klamath Falls, Oregon, and California points. In fact, the 3,859-foot siding and the adjacent spur track to the left in this view have already been taken out of service.

"ALGOMA SIGNALS"
Union Pacific Railroad
Cascade Subdivision
Algoma, Oregon
June 14, 1998

A Union Pacific Road-Railer train flies north past a signal bridge on the Cascade Line, with Upper Klamath Lake in the background. An Electro-Motive demonstration unit, SD70M #7004, is leading the way, along with a UP SD60.

"MEET AT THE SIDING"
Union Pacific Railroad
Cascade Subdivision
Wocus, Oregon
June 14, 1998

After Amtrak's Coast Starlight has rolled past, a mixed merchandise freight leaves the siding at Wocus, Oregon, as it continues south through Klamath Falls. Electro-Motive SD70M #7013 and SP SD70M #9803 power the freight.

Four Palouse River & Coulee City GP30 locomotives -- #3004, #4204, #4229, and #4109 -- rest adjacent to the ADM flour mill at Cheney, where the shortline's 108-mile, ex-Burlington Northern route to Coulee City begins. Locomotive #4109 is lettered for South Kansas & Oklahoma, a sister carrier to the PR&CC.

"CHENEY REST"
Palouse River & Coulee City Railroad
CW Subdivision
Cheney, Washington
September 19, 1999

"WINTER, HEADED FOR TOLEDO"
Southern Pacific Railroad
Valley Line
Albany, Oregon
January 9, 1990

Southern Pacific's Toledo Hauler passes the Albany, Oregon, Amtrak depot on the right and SP's important Albany Yard on the left as it skims along the Valley Line with SP GP40-2 #7952 in the lead. Less than half a mile from here, the freight will swing off the SP main and head west on the 75.8-mile Toledo Branch. The long train is en route to Georgia-Pacific's sprawling paper mill in Toledo. The TEBU slug behind the lead locomotive attests to the power required to boost heavy trains over the Coast Range, which the Toledo Hauler will soon encounter as it proceeds west.

93

"DETOUR"
Union Pacific Railroad
Oregon Trunk Subdivision
Sherar, Oregon
May 30, 1999

A detouring Union Pacific train rolls north on BNSF's Oregon Trunk Subdivision at Sherar, Oregon, on May 30, 1999. Several UP freights, as well as Amtrak trains, came over the Oregon Trunk after a serious tunnel fire on UP's ex-SP Cascade Line near Oakridge, Oregon, closed the mainline for about three days. The fire started May 27 and was finally put out on May 29. This mixed merchandise train was headed by UP units C41-8W #9425 and SD60M #6138, as well as SP locomotives SD45T-2 #9359 and SD40T-2 #8233.

UP's northbound Bend Local winds through the rocky canyon above the Deschutes River on its way back to its base yard in The Dalles. About a dozen boxcars are being hauled behind UP GP39-2s #2362 and #2574. The local operates between The Dalles and Bend -- much of the way on BNSF track -- on a one-day out, next-day back schedule.

"SPRING IN THE CANYON"
Union Pacific Railroad
Oregon Trunk Subdivision
Sherar, Oregon
April 24, 1999

"ENDLESS SCHEMES"
Burlington Northern Santa Fe Railway
Oregon Trunk Subdivision
Sherar, Oregon
May 30, 1999

A BNSF southbound comes out of Tunnel #2 on the Oregon Trunk Subdivision at Sherar, Oregon, behind four SD40-2s in a 50-50 mixture of "merger" paint schemes.

"RED LIGHTNING"
Oregon Pacific Railroad
Molalla Division
Canby, Oregon
August 6, 2000

"MARSH CROSSING"
Southern Pacific Railroad
West Side-Seghers Branch
Carnation, Oregon
September 21, 1990

Crossing a trestle at dusk, the Seghers Local heads north with two boxcar loads from the Stimson mill in Seghers, Oregon. The abbreviated train, headed by SD9 #4326, is bathed in golden light as it rumbles along on its slow return trip to Hillsboro.

"DRAWBRIDGE"
Burlington Northern Santa Fe Railway
Anacortes Branch
Whitmarsh, Washington
March 5, 1999

Behind two grimy GP39s, a local heads west on a drawbridge over Padilla Bay while on its way to serve oil refineries at Fidalgo, just east of Anacortes on BNSF's Anacortes Branch.

"RUNAWAY"
Port of Tillamook Bay Railroad
SD9 #4381
Tillamook, Oregon
August 14, 1999

"BATTERSON RUN"
Port of Tillamook Bay Railroad
Tillamook, Oregon
August 15, 1999

A frontal view of the damage suffered by POTB SD9 #4381 in a January 27, 1999, mishap in the Coast Range. The sequence of events that led to this wreck started with an eastbound freight, on its way to Banks, which suffered a derailment of a few lumber cars a couple miles west of the summit. The accident was relatively minor, and after several hours of effort the cars were re-railed. However, the train crew died on hours, so the three units in the locomotive consist -- SD9s #4381, #4405, and #4368 -- were tied up at Cochran for the night. Sometime in the darkness, the locomotive's brakes apparently failed, and the units rolled westward for two miles until they reached the site where the re-railed cars were standing on the main. The unit in the lead at the point of collision was former Southern Pacific #4381, in the brief SP-Santa Fe merger paint scheme (the only POTB locomotive so adorned). It suffered "fatal" injuries and was towed to Tillamook for salvage. The other two units were repaired and eventually returned to duty. The rail line was out of service for several days while the wreck site was cleaned up and the track repaired.

Moving slowly north through the dense coastal foliage, a pair of SD9s -- leased California Northern #210 and POTB #4432 -- pull a 12-flatcar freight to Batterson in August 1999. The Tillamook-originating train runs along the coast for most of its route, then cuts eastward into the Coast Range for another 12 miles to isolated Batterson, where it will meet a Banks-originated freight coming from the east. The two trains exchange cars there, then return to their home stations.

"SEAHAWK"
Washington Central Railroad
4th Subdivision
Warden Junction, Washington
April 8, 2000

Although officially on the roster of the Columbia Basin Railroad, Washington Central GP38 #2184 still roams the heart of Washington in WCRC colors and with the one-time regional carrier's proud "seahawk" logo. After BNSF reclaimed the Cle Elum-Pasco portion of the Stampede Pass line from Washington Central and reopened the route to through traffic, the Columbia Basin Railroad was created to haul freight on the isolated branchlines of the Moses Lake Division of the former Washington Central.

"WAITING AT THE D"
Union Pacific Railroad
Condon Branch
Gilliam, Oregon
March 22, 2000

While rain falls in the distance, three locomotives -- UP SD40-2 #3696, SP SD40T-2 #8500, and UP SD50 #5038 -- idle at the derail switch at MP 11.5, near the end of UP's Condon Branch. Later in the afternoon, the trio will be called on to haul the day's train of empty trash containers from Gilliam County's 2,000-acre landfill adjacent to the line. UP cycles the trains between Seattle and Gilliam five days a week. Most of the line, which once proceeded another 32 miles south to reach the branchline's namesake city, was torn up in 1993.

"LOS ANGELES"
Southern Pacific Railroad
SD40T-2 #8500
Condon Branch
Gilliam, Oregon
March 22, 2000

"MONTAGUE"

Central Oregon & Pacific Railroad
Siskiyou Subdivision
Montague, California
August 3, 2000

The daily southbound hauler out of Medford, Oregon -- led by three brightly-painted locomotives -- heads past California's snow-capped Mount Shasta on its way to Black Butte, California, interchange point with Union Pacific.

"THE CANADIAN"
VIA Rail
Jasper, Alberta
May 24, 2000

Soundtrack for the Rockies, with a bit of time to relax by the big rocks by the Athabasca River — hauling through the Canadian night; swaying motion, railroad dreams.

"SYMBOL OF CANADA"
Jasper National Park
Snaring River, Alberta
May 26, 2000

IV Postcards from *Canada*

*When we get to civilization, we'll have trouble making decisions.
There are no decisions now. We know what we have to do.
We have a goal: South. Every day we can get up and know
exactly what to do. Get on south.*

— Kenneth Brower, *"The Starship and the Canoe"*

"OLD AND NEW"
Canadian National Railway
Jasper, Alberta
May 24, 2000

Hauling potash, a westbound train pulled by two locomotives -- one an example of the transcontinental carrier's modern corporate image and the other reflecting an older style -- coasts to a halt in the CN yard at Jasper. After a brief pause to change crews, the freight will head west again.

When you're cold, there's nothing as welcome as sunshine
When you're dry, there's nothing as welcome as rain
When you're alone, there's nothing slower than passing time
When you're afoot, there's nothing as fast as a train.

— Mickey Newbury, "Frisco Depot," Acuff-Rose Music (BMI)

BLOOD HUNGER

We set out to ride the freights and we were not to be deterred by acts of God, perils of the rails, public enemies, public authorities acting with actual or apparent authority, customs or quarantine officials, riots, strikes or local disputes, civil commotions, hazards of war, weather conditions, mechanical failure, or acts of omission.

A few hours after dark, two eastbound freights came into the rail yard that stretched out below us, pausing to take on fresh crews.

Spider Rider watched with me from a hillside next to the Canadian National yard in Hornepayne, Ontario. There was no indication that one train or the other might be more likely to stop at the junction we were trying to get to 39 miles up the line; the trains appeared similar.

Oba was the name of the railroad junction we wanted, and we knew that trains operating over CN's transcontinental line linking Vancouver and Montreal sometimes paused there to interchange freight cars with the Algoma Central Railway. The A.C. ran a 300-mile north-south trunk straight through the rugged Ontario landscape from Sault Ste. Marie to Hearst. From Oba, we hoped to ride to the Michigan border that waited about 245 miles south.

Hornepayne was a tiny, railway-spawned community; no more than a ghost village, actually. It probably wouldn't have existed at all if not for the presence of the railroad.

Spider and I hadn't planned on being on the ground in Hornepayne, but several hours before, Canadian National police had stopped the express piggyback freight we'd been riding eastward toward Oba and "detrained" us -- in the wild. We'd been forced to walk several hot miles back along the tracks to the nearest station, and ended up at the yard facility in Hornepayne. Despite the setback, and the cops' wishes notwithstanding, we remained determined to ride a freight train out. Even if we had been inclined to avoid the freights, there was no bus service to where we were headed (and no roads either, for that matter). Passenger trains did go that way, but only three times a week, and the next eastbound was more than two days away. That was much too long for us to squat in a spot too obscure to even show up on our maps. And we steadfastly refused to consider hitchhiking: we hadn't come north to beg.

No. We came to ride Canadian freights.

But too many times on our meandering summertime journey from Seattle to Prince George and eastward from there, we'd been discovered and stopped by either provincial or railroad security forces. Our progress had been harnessed at every station and switchpoint, with more "police action" than freight action. We were playing a losing hand, it seemed -- yet through it all neither Spider nor I had mentioned the possibility of giving up our transcontinental rail journey.

That made me feel prideful, but basically there was little for either of us to go back to anyway. I'd given up an irrelevant part-time job in Oregon and set aside my college plans, for a few months, at least. With just another year to go before I could graduate, I wanted to see some definite direction behind my endeavors before pursuing it. I felt admiration for those -- like my former roommates back in Corvallis -- who seemed to know just where their lives were headed. For me, it was a constant search to figure it out. Even my long-time lover, Marie, had become just another piece in that puzzle. As much as she loved me, and as good as I felt with her, I still felt driven to explore in other directions. If it was "just a male thing," I wasn't aware of it; at least I hoped my hunger for adventure had more substance than solely that.

Spider's situation was diametrically opposed to mine: instead of "leaving behind," he was chugging toward -- new work, for one thing. He had an editor's job waiting for him in Minneapolis whenever he got around to taking it. And he was bound toward a Michigan rendezvous with the woman he was certain he wanted in his future. He also had his college degree already in hand, from prestigious Antioch College. Our situations seemed on their face to be a list of opposites, yet there was one near-blood link: we'd been born in the same hospital, in the same small Michigan town, 24 years earlier.

And we rode well together.

From that unknown hillside in Hornepayne, we stared at the two fresh trains below, then noticed a load of railroad ties on a flatcar behind the engines of the second train. It was a subtle clue, certainly, but I wondered if those ties were slated for delivery at Oba; perhaps they were to be used by the track gang that had rolled past us as we were hiking back to Hornepayne earlier. The fact that the flatcar of ties was directly behind the engines seemed to imply that the flatcar was likely to be set out soon, because trains usually switched out cars from the head end.

It was a clue to believe in. Just a thread to cling to, maybe, but to get us out of tiny Hornepayne, it was a thread when we needed it. In no time we had ourselves convinced. Those ties were bound for Oba -- where the hell else could they be going? There were precious few active stations up this stretch of nowhere, wild country track. Surely, the ties represented the manner in which the "Great Spirit" would provide for us and guide us along our chosen path.

But through all the infectious, self-convincing analyzing, I think we neglected to consult with the Great Spirit.

Or maybe we were just too eager to get rolling again.

The trains were idling, probably still in the process of changing crews, so we hurried down the hill, bathed in the bright lights illuminating the railroad yard.

"Time for your bath!" I shouted to Spider as we scrambled downhill through high, dew-soaked brush that wet us to the skin. I meant "bathe in the light," but the wet weeds supplied an extended meaning, and I didn't argue with it; I just left them both out there for Spider to chose between.

We wanted to ask a worker if one of the trains would be stopping in Oba, but at the risk of being caught again we opted not to dawdle. The vibram soles of our boots thudded hollow against steel rungs as we climbed into the shadows of the train, settling for the second level of an empty tri-level auto-carrier. It would be a ride open to the Canadian breezes, but we had no alternative. We needed hiding shelter, and as far as we could see, virtually everything else -- on both trains -- appeared to be boxcars, sealed tight.

At 1:05 a.m., our chosen train left the switching yard at Hornepayne. As the freight crawled away from the settlement, I was overcome with the wine of our apparent victory. We had eluded capture by the rail police, who scant hours earlier had threatened us with deportation back to the United States if we dared to grab a freight again.

"To hell with deportation!" I jubilantly shouted at Spider, my voice rising above the slow squealing of steel wheels on steel rails. Feeling boundless, I climbed up the softly swaying auto-rack ladder to the top floor as the train gained momentum for its eastward run.

I put my back on the cool steel floor and opened my senses to the sky and stars. The view, and the rocking sensation of the accelerating train, turned overwhelming. Soon Spider came to the top, wondering why I hadn't come back; curious to know what I had discovered. That was what I had hoped for. Like climbing down from the Moose Jaw trestle and jogging alongside the Winnipeg grain train days earlier, the clear purity of the stars over North America was something to be shared.

The Canadian night wrapped us in an entrancing spell. The aurora borealis glowed so brightly that beams from green spotlights appeared to be dancing across the sky, illuminating the atmosphere vividly. There were no city lights anywhere to diminish the visual impact of the electric carpet of stars.

We remained splayed on our backs while the quickening roar of howling wind and spinning wheels became too loud to permit talking. In silence we stared, watching for meteor flashes and reveling in the cool breezes that rippled over us.

It was a maximum ride. Overcome by the experience, we boldly rose and stood atop our car, focused only on the magic of the Canadian wilderness rolling past. There was an immediate wash of perspective, and my lack of income meant nothing: I gladly would have traded all the money I'd make in the next five years in exchange for the power of that night (although later Spider would jokingly say, "That's an easy promise for you to offer -- you probably won't make any money in the next five years.")

Slowly, however, the exuberance spawned by the sweet freight ride began to wear off, and the reality of cold air against our damp clothing began to set in. It was difficult to tell how fast the train was racing in the blackness, but the swift air was increasingly wintry, and the night was long yet ahead of us. It wouldn't be wise -- or healthy -- to remain unprotected in the constant wind atop that steel platform.

I was beginning to shiver uncontrollably, but had no sleeping bag to crawl into. Feeling cocky and tough, we'd both come up top without any of our sleeping gear.

It wasn't merely a matter of going down to the second level of the car to retrieve our sleeping bags. The auto-carrier's rocking ladder had become a slick, intimidating threat, and to attempt to descend at the speed the train was pushing -- especially since our bodies were getting a bit numbed with the chill -- represented a potentially greater risk than the deepening cold.

Moving from one level to another on an auto-carrier, even with the car at rest, was no simple feat. It required dexterity and a sure grip. Once on the ladder, you had to twist like a snake into a passageway roughly four feet high, and at the point where the rungs of the ladder intersected the second level, a slip could mean a 10-foot drop between two freight cars.

In essence, we felt we had little choice but to stay where we were -- unless we became convinced that death would result if we remained any longer.

Choose your poison.

Signal towers were plainly visible over the top of the train. We could see the colored beams of the railway's "traffic lights" diffused by diesel smoke, but always the color beckoning us was green -- a bright emerald green to rival the Northern Lights above. Pretty as it looked, its meaning was not at all comforting: the train was being highballed down the line, with no stops, no orders even to slow down.

So far, we had not heard the wheels clacking through the diamond of the rail crossing with the Algoma Central at Oba, nor had we seen any sign of a town. In vain we listened for the hum of the engines to alter in pitch, signaling a deceleration for the yard limits of Oba.

The station had to be near, but constantly ahead of us shined the grim reality: Highball. Highball. Highball. Green signal lights winked at us about every two miles, mocking, laughing at us through chilled teeth. Green lights on cold metal poles hurtled past, sending us sailing express down the line, into the next block of mainline track, and the next, and the next …

After more than an hour of movement, I was relieved to notice a distant amber glow instead of green. It meant one of two things: either our freight was going to meet another train and would be diverted onto a siding, or the train was approaching Oba.

It was 2:30 a.m.

A few minutes later, our eastbound pulled onto a desolate siding. Except for the colorful glow of distant signal towers and the headlights that pointed the way for the locomotives, there were no lights around us, in any direction.

As the freight slowed, Spider and I crouched alert and anxious for a chance to get down to the second floor to reach our warming gear. The bitter cold had hobbled us to the point that we needed to wait for the train to come to a full stop before descending the ladder.

As we stood stretching and gathering ourselves for the climb down, the headlights of an oncoming train raced toward us. In a blur, the interior lamplights of a warm, westbound VIA passenger train glided past in deliverance.

Back on the second level, with our freight train for the moment idling peacefully, we turned our attention to a new gamble: should we abandon the train and assume we were close enough to walk into Oba? It seemed a relatively safe bet to make. Oba was just 39 miles from Hornepayne, so if we'd averaged about 40 miles per hour, as seemed reasonable, and if we figured actual running time at 70 minutes -- allowing for the slower pace at the beginning as the train pulled out of the yard, and at the end as the train slowed before entering the siding -- we figured we'd traveled somewhere between 45 and 50 miles. Subtracting the 39 miles from that left between six and 11 miles, give or take a few. We

could hike that without much difficulty. Hell, it would be fun!

Yet I still found it hard to accept that we could have already passed Oba. Surely we would have seen some indication of the town if that were true. I was fervently hoping Oba was only a mile or two farther down the tracks to the east, and hoping the train had been moving deceptively slowly all along. In any case, after the chilling ride, we agreed we needed to stand on solid ground again, with no breezes buffeting us.

There wasn't a lot of time for discussion. No more than a minute after the VIA train flashed past on the main, the freight's engines were already idling up, pulling the slack out of a long line of freight cars and preparing to smoke back onto the main track.

Spider went down the rungs first, while I paused momentarily, waiting for space on the narrow ladder.

The locomotives were accelerating surprisingly rapidly. Spider reached the gravel, but by then the train was moving almost too fast; I dropped down my pack and scrambled. Spider swung up his flashlight and beamed it onto the ground, trying to give me an extra edge to find my footing as the rocky rough ground below spun weirdly with the rolling train.

In another moment, I hopped off to the ground, safe. Spider and I stood side by side in the blackness at the remote siding, watching for a minute or two as the remaining freight cars rushed past.

After the caboose cleared, all sound dropped away, and when the red light marking the rear of the long train faded from view, we were alone.

It was cold, black, and quiet. We were off the train. But where?

I walked to the signal tower a few boxcar lengths ahead and climbed up. I wanted to be off the ground, away from the wet ground and the fear of wandering bears.

"I'll feel a lot easier when I can see where we are and get a look at the terrain," I said, not wanting to admit I was afraid we might encounter a bear. Spider joined me on the tower, not admitting to any concerns. After a few minutes standing aimlessly in the blackness, we climbed back onto the tracks.

Bringing out his flashlight, Spider said simply, "Are you ready for the flashlight of truth?" A milepost indicator stenciled on the base of the tower would reveal our location.

"Let's get it over with," I said.

He clicked the beam on, and the truth was grim. Incredibly, we had overshot Oba by 26 miles.

We climbed up again, and sat silently on the narrow platform near the top of the signal tower, waiting out the night.

Dawn came slowly. As the sky finally lightened, we could see more clearly what we already knew: we were at the eastern end of a long railway siding in the wilds of Canada. From the point where the side track joined with the main, there was one shiny set of rails that continued out of sight. That was all. As far as we could see in any direction, there were trees, brush, rocks, and swamp. There were no houses, no roads, no buildings, no airplanes overhead even. It was utter isolation.

Twenty-six miles back to the west was Oba. In the other direction, the next station that our maps showed, Elsas, was apparently even farther.

So we headed westward along the rails, entertaining the belief that we could proceed afoot to Oba. It would take at least 10 hours of hiking, but time was not a limiting factor. Whatever it took was what we'd give it. No big deal. And there was always the possibility of catching a slow train going our way. The uncertainty created mystery, and the mystery wove adventure. It was a mixture that fueled us.

After no more than half a mile of walking, however, the sole of Spider's right boot came loose. It flapped outward with every step he took, forcing him to walk awkwardly and slowing our pace. He finally had to stop and rig a fix, using a piece of wire he found along the roadbed. The wire held the sole closed, crudely. We continued westward.

By the time we had gone about a mile -- roughly half the length of the two-mile nowhere siding we had been deposited on -- bugs began to annoy us. Responding to some signal of heat or light, tiny black flies rose up from the weeds and swarmed in growing clouds around our heads. Then they began to bite. Big mosquitoes soon joined in, and we had to keep moving, swinging our arms to try to keep them away from us.

We had assumed we'd cheated the elements when we bailed out from the frigid freight train, but we were discovering that we remained exposed; it was just that "the elements" were a bit different on the ground. It quickly became clear that the airborne pests were a bigger threat than we ever would have considered. We slapped on a healthy dose of Cutters, the insect repellent, but it proved almost totally ineffective against the flying parasites.

The bugs were ravenous. It was possible that we were the first humans on foot there in months, perhaps years, and the smell of unfamiliar meat seemed to be sending them into a frenzy.

There was nowhere to hide.

I was uneasy about it, but I wasn't seriously concerned. So when I saw Spider take off running to avoid a large dragonfly that buzzed toward his face, I laughed. I chided him for not knowing that the dragonflies were harmless. They would leave us alone, I told him, and in fact might even help drive off some of the smaller bugs. That had been my experience in other backwoods spots I'd been unsheltered in, during trips to different parts of states such as Wisconsin and Iowa.

In another moment, however, several huge dragonflies began to float around me, and my laughing stopped. One dragonfly landed long enough to tear a tiny bite out of my neck, bringing me to a shocked, anxious realization: We had landed in a place where the rules were different. The Ontario railroad siding was alien to anything we had encountered before, and it was clear that all the tiny winged creatures hovering there were literally out for our blood. We expected as much from the mosquitoes and the black flies, although certainly not at such a voracious level. But it was almost stunning to me that even dragonflies rushed to feed at our life-juices; even the elegant dragonflies would show no mercy!

I knocked away a buzzing dragonfly and clapped my hand to the back of my neck, coming away with several dead black flies. But for every dead one there were more waiting. They were endless, and they were everywhere.

The challenge had become a nightmare. Attempting to walk another 25 miles in such conditions would be intolerable, possibly suicidal. It seemed that if we were left exposed indefinitely, we could literally be eaten alive.

We reached the western end of the siding and discovered a low wooden shanty, perhaps 10 feet long by six feet wide, with two plexi-glass windows and a wooden door. Next to the shanty was a small cement booth that contained a radio-telephone designed to link train crews with a dispatcher somewhere. On the far side of the gray, weather-beaten structure was a metal signpost with the station name posted in bold, black letters:

DISHNISH

The name struck us as ludicrous.

"Dishnish!" Spider snorted derisively. The name was almost comical, and we both laughed at the first reading. But our situation was anything but humorous: since hiking was out, we were stuck there indefinitely. Maybe until we got lucky and another train stopped on the passing track.

The shanty door was unlocked, although we were prepared to force our way in if it had not been. Happily for us, CN apparently realized there was no danger of vandalism since there were no towns or roads for miles in any direction. Still, if we were merely to open the door and casually enter the small shelter, many of the bugs forming hellish halos around us and clinging to our clothing and hair would be carried inside, and we would have accomplished little: there would be no refuge from the biting beasts.

What we finally figured out was basic enough. We backed off about 30 paces from the entrance, and swept the bugs from our clothing and hair. Then we raced for the door, burst through, and slammed it closed. This procedure left most of the bugs in our wake. Sprinting was the only way we

had to get the bugs away from us, and of course that solution was effective only fleetingly. But a fleeting moment was all we required, and it worked well enough.

Inside, there was one thin wooden bench and a dusty cement floor, but it was a haven. We could stay dry and virtually bug-free within, and remain sheltered from the cool winds blowing through southern Ontario.

The hours passed. I slept, Spider slept. It rained a bit. The sky was gray, gloomy. We didn't speak much.

Only the intermittent need to urinate drove us from the shelter. We took unspoken turns on the bench, one leaving the floor to replace the other during dashes outside to take a jogging piss or to briefly listen in on the CN radio chatter at the booth outside, where we hoped to pick up a scrap of information alerting us to a train being diverted onto the siding at Dishnish.

The electronic link to the distant dispatcher was our only connection with the rest of the world, although the assault of the bugs, at some level, was proof of a common bond; something potentially shared with every human being. It was comforting to know the radio link was there.

But no helpful news came over the wire, and time rolled by almost deliriously. The numerous insect bites we'd sustained apparently had taken a toll; our systems seemed drugged by insect venom. We lolled about on floor or bench, drifting in and out of deep, fevered sleep.

We waited, and endured. We had no choice.

Since our early-morning arrival at Dishnish, two eastbound and three westbound freights had raced through, their blurring pace making a mockery of any idea we might have had about catching a ride out of there. In the dusty silence, the high-pitched whine of oncoming freights rattling along the steel rail outside penetrated our slumber and stirred us long enough to pay attention as trains descended on Dishnish and blasted through at 60 miles an hour. Spider and I would glance recognition at each other -- determining there was no chance -- and then our heads would drop back down into exhausted semiconsciousness even before the ending caboose cleared our pathetic shanty.

At some point, we considered trying to contact the dispatcher, explain that we were stranded at Dishnish out of food, low on water, and under siege by nature.

But that was a solution of final resort. We figured we would be arrested if they had to come out to rescue us, and besides, to be rescued implied we had been beaten -- a humiliating, unacceptable finale to our ongoing duel with the rail police and the elements.

So the hours kept mounting: 18, 24, 30. A number of freight trains blew through at 50 or 60 mph. Night came, and then daylight again. We were nearly out of water. I began to consider the possibility that some track laborers might find our bones in the shanty someday.

Finally, we heard another distant train -- but this one sounded different. There was a tangible change in the pitch of the engines, indicating slowing, perhaps a pending stop; clearly, at least, this one wasn't going to scream through like all the other trains had. We grabbed our packs and ran from the shanty to a hiding spot behind some gigantic rocks, steeling ourselves against the damned bugs. We were prepared to run for the train, even if it was rolling faster than we normally would have wanted to risk. Poison again: die quickly by the wheel, perhaps, or slowly by insect venom and thirst.

In a few minutes, a long, eastbound freight came past, hauling boxcars, auto-racks, and gondolas. It pulled smoothly onto the siding and hissed to a stop. We raced from behind our rock cover and reached an empty boxcar.

Taking the eastbound meant getting to Oba was out, of course, but we had long since realized we would have to take the train that came first, regardless of its direction. There would be other avenues into Michigan.

Ironically, it was another westbound VIA passenger train that provided us with a ticket out of trouble, by coming through at precisely the right time to force the eastbound freight to take the siding. VIA Rail! It had been the butt of many of our jokes, as we'd ridiculed the conservative nature of passenger trains numerous times during our Trans-Canada freight expedition. But here was VIA, saving our butts again.

The mixed freight train carried us away from Dishnish, and ahead to Capreol. Triumphantly, we rode CN freights from there all the way to Toronto.

Neither cops nor bugs caught up to us again.

"HEART OF THE ROCKIES"
Canadian National Railway
Jasper, Alberta
May 25, 2000

A CN stack train pulls west out of Jasper, bound for Vancouver, British Columbia.

Just the ice view from our mountaintop and the cider and rolling with The Canadian; sweet fireplace nights, mountains turning rosy. Plenty of sun here, never enough but plenty, and no rain since Vancouver. A few more nights under Canadian stars …

"INTERMODAL DESIGN"
Canadian National Railway
Jasper, Alberta
May 2000

"SKEENA"
VIA Rail
Jasper, Alberta
May 24, 2000

The tri-weekly "Skeena" passenger train, behind colorful VIA F40PH-2 #6454, leaves Jasper on its run to Prince Rupert, British Columbia.

113

"HALFWAY TO PORT ALBERNI"

RailAmerica
Esquimalt & Nanaimo District
Little Qualicum Falls, Vancouver Island, British Columbia
May 26, 2000

Three RailAmerica locomotives, led by #3877, pull 24 boxcars around a rainy corner of Vancouver Island. The train is headed to an inland paper mill at Port Alberni, British Columbia.

"LEAVING BANFF"
Canadian Pacific Railroad
Laggan Subdivision
Banff, Alberta
August 25, 2000

"RAIN IN THE ROCKIES"
Canadian Pacific Railroad
Laggan Subdivision
Banff, Alberta
August 26, 2000

"NORTH COAST LIMITED, FADING"
Washington Central Railroad
4th Subdivision
Warden, Washington
April 8, 2000

WCRC #201, an ex-Northern Pacific Railway boxcar, displays aging colors and obsolete slogans on a storage track in Warden, Washington. The North Coast Limited was one of NP's crack passenger trains during the 1950s.

"VENERABLE SPIRIT"
Milwaukee Road
Super Dome #55
Tillamook, Oregon
September 1989

Epilogue

Lind, Washington

"
Yesterday,

I heard they shut the trains down;

The ones that ran

By the field where I would play

They said folks want new and faster transportation

It's just like me

I'll be obsolete one day.
"

— Bob Seger, "Railroad Days," Gear Music Pub. (ASCAP)

"GHOST BRIDGE, MILWAUKEE ROAD"
Lind, Washington
April 8, 2000

Directly west of Lind, Washington, Burlington Northern Santa Fe's single-tracked Lakeside Subdivision (between Spokane and Pasco) passes through the concrete remains of what was once a mainline bridge on the Milwaukee Road's route to Tacoma.

ON THE BRIDGE, *Gone*

Sure miss the Milwaukee Road. Last weekend I took off for the north to visit some MR remnants at Lind and Othello and Warden and Royal City. It was poignant, sad and sweet. These are towns where sections of the former transcontinental mainline were retained, turned into a shortline to serve a handful of serious customers along the route. So here and there, short stretches of the Milwaukee Road's tracks remain. Here and there, signal towers still stand, with the signal heads removed. But it's touching to see the old milepost signs on lonely vigil. There, on a rickety, 20-mile shortline, are dramatic mileposts: 1,960, for example. That's how far the Milwaukee Road had stretched from St. Paul or Minneapolis or Milwaukee, wherever the headquarters once was.

In 1977, I rode the Milwaukee line from Montevideo, Minnesota, to Missoula, Montana, and foolishly switched over to Burlington Northern when I got to Missoula, because BN ran so many more trains than the Milwaukee Road. The ratio was probably about 15-1, and I guess I was in a rush, impatient to get on to the next place. Now I see the torn away roadbed in open calling places and wished to God I had stuck with the Milwaukee Road to keep going west; wished I could say, hey, I once rode freight here.

Ever been through Lind, Washington? The concrete bridge pillars remain where the Milwaukee Road's Pacific Coast Extension crossed a BN line, but now the decking is long gone, so you have these huge monoliths in the middle of nowhere, truly an amazing scene, and I went there to photograph it. Dreaming of a chance long past, craving a lost possible memory of a Milwaukee Road ride through there, and to the end of the line …

"AFTERMATH"
Northwestern Pacific Railroad
Fortuna, California
July 31, 2000

Looking north along the rails of the Northwestern Pacific Railroad. The tracks, out of service since flooding in 1996, may yet be reborn if sufficient funding to rebuild the line between Willits and Eureka is realized.